BEYOND THE

SUNSET

MALCOLM CAMPBELL

SOLO SAIL AROUND THE

WORLD

LIFE'S CHALLENGES AND LIVING YOUR DREAM

Some reviews:

"A fascinating story well written. The autobiography is interwoven with the journal of a solo circumnavigation. Growing up in unique circumstances in South Africa and Rhodesia, crossing oceans in a home built boat and the love for his partner and family and of course the companionship of his dog Bebe. It's the story of a life lived fully and well outside the boundaries of most people's comfort zones. An easy but hugely satisfying read." August 2020.

"I finished the book in just 2 sittings! It was a fascinating read. Malcolm went through so much, good and bad. Amazing achievement, great book, well done, have already recommended it to many people." October 2020.

"Reading Malcolm's book shows where a person's drive comes from, and demonstrates how hard-earned skills can make dreams happen. An extraordinary journey on what turned out to be an extraordinary boat, sailed by a very special kind of sailor. Superbly told story, and the enormity of the achievement is brought home in the detailed daily account of events, especially for a non-sailor. Bravo Malcolm

upon the Circumnavigation, a safe return and of course the book." October 2020.

"An easy to read fascinating autobiography where you are taken on a journey through this amazing man's life and his solo sail around the world. A must read for anyone who enjoys adventure and admires courage and resilience. Definitely a page turner which I could not put down!" September 2020.

"A well written story. I felt that I was actually there with Malcolm. I couldn't put the book down. What a brave thing to do. Thoroughly recommend reading it. Very enjoyable." September 2020.

"This story is a "must read" for all sailors, and for anyone who admires people with skill, courage, discipline and resilience. Malcolm gives a full account of his solo circum-navigation of the globe in his yacht "Grace". And, to make it all the more enjoyable, we learn of his family and earlier life which is full of highs and lows like the rest of us. It is hard to believe that anyone in an old 38ft wooden boat, with a dog, could achieve what Malcolm achieved at age 70, and that's why you will enjoy every page of his story." August 2020.

Dedication

Many people helped me achieve my dream to solo sail around the world.

Fiona and Neil, my two children were responsible in raising money to help in re-building the mast and to those who gave, I thank you all. You were my salvation at a very hard time.

Marilyn my partner for 22 years whose support for, and during, the 2 years 9 months voyage kept me linked to home and updating my family and friends on a regular basis of my progress. I thank her for her love and loyalty and her patience and hard work in helping me with this book.

CONTENTS

CONTENTS

CONTENTS

CONTENTS

DAY BY DAY WE SAILED

ALWAYS WEST

INTO THE SUNSET

AND BEYOND

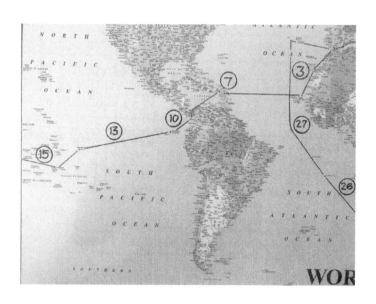

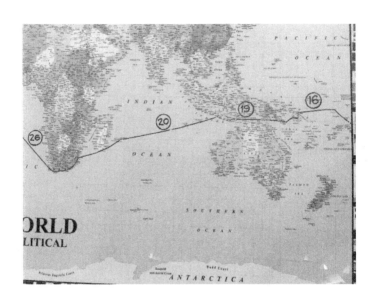

Prologue

"*Well you see*", said Ted *"I am dying and the doctors have not given me that much time."* I stood before Ted in his front garden, alongside a tarpaulin covered wooden yacht which Marilyn had come to see. I had heard of this boat from a friend of Ted's, who implied that Ted would virtually give it away to right person. This person should be a sailor with experience in woodwork.

He had previously sailed the boat after having built it some 20 years ago, and subsequently moved it to his garden to raise the sides and give the it more head room. Shortly after this he was diagnosed with spine cancer and unfortunately had to cease work on the boat.

I am a furniture maker and had a small workshop on a farm near East Meon in the beautiful South Downs. I had previously sailed two boats (which I had built) across the Atlantic. This satisfied Ted's criteria and he felt that I was the right person to take on the boat. The only snag was that with a recent divorce and two children in higher education I had very little money and lived in a caravan on the farm where I worked. To ensure very little disruption to the lives of my children, I had given my house to my ex-wife.

Marilyn was the new lady in my life. We had been seeing each other for a year and she was quite aware of my love for boats and sailing. Our first sight of this boat with the new planking still rough, unfaired and glue runs down the sides was not impressive, but I could see that once the hull was sanded and painted this boat would be most attractive, as her lines were pretty in a classical style. I could tell by the look on Marilyn's face that she was not convinced and did not believe that I would buy it! I had said to Marilyn on the drive to see this boat at Bosham (near Chichester) that I basically was not really interested in a wooden boat, especially a home built one, which now after 20 years Ted had raised the sides. It did not sound very appealing. Ted removed the covers and said, "*Go inside the boat and take a look and when you have finished you will find me in my house with the kettle on.*"

Marilyn and I climbed the ladder on to the newly laid half deck. The cockpit, cabin and the rest of the deck had not yet been built. The interior of the boat was bare with no flooring, partitions or any structure that one would expect below the deck. By the look on Marilyn's face I could see that she was unimpressed and never thought that I would buy this boat. Now, on close inspection of the bare interior, I quickly realised that this boat had been built by Ted with great skill and knowledge to a very high professional standard. It was love at first sight, not a doubt existed in my mind. I had to have this boat! Ted had explained previously that the engine, sails, fuel tanks, portholes, ropes, anchors, cooker and all other fittings were in storage in boxes. We went back inside the house and I said to Ted, "*Ted I like your boat and would like to buy it but I have no money at this time*" to which he replied "*Pay me what you can, when you can and take the boat away when you can afford it. I know you are the person for my boat!"* Little did I know that day, this boat would sail me across the Atlantic Ocean six times, four of which would be solo, and then take me on a solo voyage around the world.

BEYOND THE SUNSET

1

Kefalonia and near tragedy

Kefalonia is the island on which Marilyn and I have lived since 2003 which we first sailed to on Grace from America so that I could take up employment. It is a beautiful island and many will be familiar with it from the film "Captain Corelli's Mandolin".

I left Drapano dock, which is the other side of the lagoon opposite Argostoli, on the morning of 15th September 2015, after saying goodbye to Marilyn and fifteen or so well wishers and dear friends who were there to wish me luck and bon voyage. With me was Beebee, my lovely dog.

This was the start of my circumnavigation on Grace which I felt was well prepared with new sails, electronics and more equipment than I would normally carry. One new addition was a satellite tracker which would enable my position to be plotted on my website. I had set this up so that my followers could see my position on a daily basis and promote the charity that is linked to my circumnavigation, to raise money for cancer research. The tracker would also enable Marilyn and I to send short text messages via satellite to one another, irrespective of where I am on the planet. Departures like this I always find very emotional but at the same time quite stressful. Soon Marilyn and all my friends would be left behind and I would find myself alone at sea. This was the start of a two years voyage, not really knowing what lay ahead as we endeavoured to circle the globe in what most modern yachtsman would call a primitive boat. I was able to carry on talking to Marilyn for the next twenty five miles on the telephone, but at this point I lost the signal but not before I was able to tell her that I loved her.

Beebee would not toilet or eat during the following 24 hours which is quite understandable. The weather was not unpleasant and I hoped to make Regio de Calabria, in the Messina Straights on the Italian mainland within three days, a distance of 290 miles. We arrived there without incident but on learning the high cost of a stay in the marina, I decided to carry on to Milazzo on the north coast of Sicily.

Bad weather forced us to heave-to for 24 hours so we arrived in Sicily a day later than anticipated, on the 23rd September. Here we waited four days for the wind to swing into the east before we could leave. The forecast for the next six days was easterly winds 10 to 15 knots, ideal sailing winds. Over the next five days, whilst trying to cross over to Menorca, the forecast proved far from accurate and most of the time the wind was north west swinging to south west. This made for slow uncomfortable sailing, the boat being wet most of the time from the rough seas.

KEFALONIA AND NEAR TRAGEDY

On the 29th September the strong southerly wind became gale force and I was forced to heave-to under triple reefed mainsail and a very small staysail. The seas quickly became rough and very short, as well as steep and violent which is typical in a Mediterranean gale due to the relatively shallow water. I had little control of Grace and even though I had set her up to heave-to, she was still being thrown from pillar to post. At about 02:00 hours on 30th September I was awoken from an exhausted sleep by a large explosion of noise and water. To my horror when I went up on deck I was confronted by a vision of utter destruction. The deck was criss-crossed with ropes and rigging wires, the stanchions and the push-pit were bent and mangled and worst of all, the mast, boom and sails were gone, having been swept overboard!

I could see the whiteness of the sails, lying about two metres deep under the boat and I could feel the hammering of the mast against the hull, all of which were still attached to the boat by the rigging. Waves of fear and panic were washing over me and I thought that this was the beginning of a sequence that would result in the sinking of Grace. I was both terrified and shocked, unable to think what to do. It became necessary to try and switch off my wildly over working mind and go into an automatic robotic mode, thinking only of what I had to do minute by minute. It was obvious that the mast must be cut away quickly before it holed the boat, so I began to cut the ropes and rigging wires which had to be done whilst lying flat on the violently pitching deck in these mountainous seas, an

almost impossible task in these extreme conditions.
Somehow, after about forty minutes, the last halyard was
cut and the mast and all my new sails were on the way to
the bottom of the Mediterranean sea.

I stayed below in my bunk, feeling absolutely
wretched, just letting the boat drift in the violent waves.
The nearest land was Menorca, about fifty miles away and
there was no point in trying to motor in these extreme
conditions. I decided to wait until things improved before
getting under way. At 10:00 hours both the wind and the
sea had calmed down sufficiently for me to start motoring
for Menorca. Through the day the waves and the wind
became much calmer, allowing me to arrive four miles
from Menorca at about midnight. By now my diesel fuel
was finished, so there was no alternative but to ask the
coast guard, on my hand-held radio, for a tow into Mahon.

Within an hour a large gleaming orange twenty five
metre rescue vessel appeared out of the darkness, coming
as near alongside as the heaving seas would allow. A
monkeys fist was thrown to me followed by a towing bridal
which I attached to the bollards on Grace. I was talking to
the captain of the rescue vessel using my hand-held radio
which I had charged during the day, so the operation went
well, not withstanding that the crew were very
professional. We were towed at a steady five knots into
Mahon. It was almost surreal to be quietly making our way
slowly up the long channel to the dock in the early
morning hours surrounded by the lights of Mahon. I was
asked to come aboard the rescue vessel to do the

paperwork, where I met the well-spoken young captain at which time I complimented him on the efficiency of his crew. He asked me how strong the wind had been, to which I replied, "*A strong gale.*" He corrected me saying that they had received wide reports of wind speeds in excess of seventy knots. The island had suffered extensive damage to property and many trees had been blown down and this evidence I saw for myself the next day.

Unbeknown to me, Marilyn had learnt of the bad storm in this part of the Mediterranean and having not received any transmissions for a few days had become extremely worried for my safety.

What now? In an email that I had sent to Marilyn I said "*Well, Beebee, Grace and I will carry on and I will re-build the mast and boom. I know my budget does not allow for this, but I really have no choice, so I will let the future look after itself. It seems that to be a member of the solo circumnavigation club requires high membership fees and it is not meant to be easy. I am sorry that I have caused so much worry to you and the family but on the bright side, we survive to sail another day.*"

The dock to which we were taken to was part of a very large government boat yard. This yard had mostly private boats of all descriptions, stored or being worked on and private contractors and cranes were free to come and go. On enquiry I found that the yard offered a place where I could both live and work on Grace out of the water. The costs were surprisingly inexpensive and furthermore, I could use a private crane to lift the boat out of the water, at a very competitive rate.

Two days later Grace was safely chocked up on the hard-standing and I was busy looking at used masts and other equipment.

It soon became clear that there was little that was suitable so I found a timber supplier on the island who had beautiful kiln-dried North American Douglas fir. Woodwork is my business and I love working in wood, so during the following three months I had a very enjoyable time building a 12 metres long wooden mast and a boom.

Building a new 12 metre mast for Grace

The numerous stainless steel attachments and fittings required on a sailing yacht, were made by a wonderful small workshop and were quite happy to weld up fittings which I had made.

Grace's new mast

Amongst my fellow residents were four other English speaking yachties and I soon struck up friendships with all of them including two Spanish yachtsmen. They showed me great kindness by taking me to town to buy glue, paint and fastenings and offering help whenever they could. Beebee was happy and enjoyed lots of attention from the other residents in the yard and to this day I have very fond memories of the Mahon boat yard, the total professionalisms of the rescue captain and crew and my most enjoyable stay there.

Grace chocked up in Mahon and fitted with new mast

We re-launched Grace on the 21st December
having completed all the repairs to the hull and the deck.
She looked splendid with her new mast and shiny new
stainless steel rigging, which was supplied by a local
English rigger who offered a totally professional service. I
had sent for a new mainsail from China and the other sails

were bought second-hand on the island.

The next morning I took on diesel fuel and left for the very beautiful anchorage at La Mola fort, where I spent two days fitting sails and finalising the repairs, getting Grace ocean ready in the breath taking beauty and solitude of the anchorage.

Grace at anchorage at La Mola fort

KEFALONIA AND NEAR TRAGEDY

On completion of the work, we sailed for Porto Colom on the island of Majorca, about sixty miles away, where I enjoyed Christmas with an old friend, Geoff who I had met on a previous stopover. Geoff lived on his boat in the anchorage and was a popular character amongst the locals.

On the second of January I sailed for Almerimar on the mainland, arriving there ten days later. This is my favourite marina on the Spanish coast and Marilyn was able to fly in and spend ten days with me. We had a wonderful time together, exploring the area in a rented car and enjoying each other's company. All too soon, the time passed and I had to take Marilyn to the airport and return to the boat to make immediate preparations to sail to Gibraltar, which is approximately 100 miles away. It was very sad having to say goodbye to Marilyn who I would not see again for eighteen months.

I set sail for Gibraltar with a feeling of inner satisfaction, having turned disaster around, so that our circumnavigation was now back on track, but also sadness at knowing it would be a long time before Marilyn and I would be together again.

2

A return to the Atlantic

Tuesday 8th March 2016

The log entry at 16:00 hours reads *"Cape Spartel on port beam, wind 2 knots westerly, sea light 1 metre swell. Back in the Atlantic again."*

We have just motored through the Straights of Gibraltar which is about thirty miles from Gibraltar. This being my third approach from the Mediterranean into the Atlantic. Transiting the Straights is always done with trepidation as the current is consistently strong and normally against a westerly passage causing strong overfalls and at times big seas due to the wind against the current situation.

So here we are, on the way to try and circumnavigate the planet in Grace, my forty year old wooden 38 foot sailboat. If all goes well this will be a two year circumnavigation, via the Panama Canal through the Pacific Ocean, across the Indian Ocean, around the Cape of South Africa, then back to Europe via Gibraltar. I sense the drama of the moment and a fear of the unknown. Will I be up to it? The boat can definitely handle it as she is strong and well built, but can I, at my age, handle the hard times that lie ahead? Bad weather, sleepless nights and fatigue that lead to a loss of concentration resulting in potential disaster?

I have my faithful dog Beebee with me, who has sailed the Atlantic before on a double crossing.

I am at the same time excited, nervous and filled with apprehension, already missing Marilyn terribly and the wonderful life we share in Kefalonia.

But now as the light dims and we turn south for the Canaries about eight hundred miles away, the sea is calm and the Moroccan lights are beginning to twinkle through the evening twilight.

By 18:00 hours we are enjoying a beautiful sail, on course at four knots on a gentle undulating sea.

All our systems are functioning perfectly and Beebee my ever loyal dog is having a snooze in the cockpit after her first Atlantic dinner and a successful trip to the toilet on the foredeck.

We are seeing the occasional trawler which means that I cannot sleep for more than thirty minutes at a time and further off the coast is a steady flow of shipping, about one an hour. This shows up on my A.I.S. plotter, a type of radar, which identifies a ship, shows its relative position, its heading and speed.

This is a wonderful welcome back into the Atlantic and my spirits are soaring as Grace heads south at a steady urge to cover mileage. Aries my mechanical wind pilot, which steers the boat automatically, is working to perfection, which means I barely have to touch the helm, so allowing me to sleep with relative peace of mind, whilst Grace surges on, unattended through the night.

Gibraltar to Canaries
08:00 hours Wednesday 9th March 2016
N 35 10 W 06 59
sea rolly
wind calm
88 miles from Cape Spartel motoring

We motored all morning on a smooth sea in bright sun the sky very blue and cloudless.

At 17:00 hours I write in the log that the wind has returned and is now blowing at ten knots and we are enjoying a splendid afternoon sail. At 22:00 hours the wind is now increasing and a reef is required, this means that the sail area must be reduced to keep the boat manageable and safe. Within two hours I have to put in another reef, the wind is up to thirty knots and the sea is rough. Aries requires frequent attention and the visibility is reduced to half a mile due to frequent rain showers.

Nevertheless, we are managing to keep to four knots in this north west wind, which is blowing on our starboard quarter. The sea is now rough with the swell at two metres but as it is from behind, it is not too uncomfortable for Grace. She is handling it well and sailing with great confidence with her new mast, a smaller rig than we had when we left Kefalonia.

09:00 hours Thursday 10th March 2016
N 33 54 W 08 41
Grand Canaria 490 miles
sea rough 2 metres
wind NW 15 to 30 knots
double reefed speed 4 knots

At noon I write in the log that the wind seems to be dropping, which I am very pleased about. We have made over 110 miles since noon yesterday which is very satisfying, so it seems we are off to a good start. This leaves about 480 miles to Grand Canaria, so in theory we could be there in about five days or so.

I record in the log at 17:00 hours contrary to what I had written previously, the wind has increased to thirty knots. Aries my auto-pilot, will not steer in this wind strength so this leaves me no choice but to heave-to, which means I back the sails and we drift. This is considered a safe manoeuvre in bad weather and not too uncomfortable. The boat will lie at about 50 degrees to the wind and the waves. At this time I also notice that the engine mountings are loose, requiring tightening and re-aligning once we get to Grand Canaria.

Beebee of course is not happy in these conditions, as I have to keep her down below, only allowing her on deck in her harness when she needs to go to the toilet. This is often a difficult procedure on a deck which is sloping steeply at thirty degrees and bouncing up and down. She has to be very selective at which spot she chooses to relieve herself, as it seems some spots don't have the right smell, so we have to endure her circling a small area on the deck while she smells and examines it for up to three minutes, all in rain and wind swept spray. Only when she is completely satisfied with the location, will she do the business. Unfortunately, this procedure is not without risk to both of us.

Friday 11th March 2016

09:00 hours sea rough wind light and variable

warm and sunny

heading 240 magnetic

Our run since yesterday noon is only fifty one miles, which is to be expected, as we were hove-to overnight. During the morning the wind remained very light but at noon it picked up to an easy 10 knot breeze, so we are now enjoying a very pleasant sail over a more settled sea. I spent the afternoon tightening up the engine mounts, so feeling very pleased with myself as working on the engine at sea requires a strong stomach. I do not normally get seasick, but working with my head in the bilge does test my sea legs.

Saturday 12th March
09:00 hours N 32 29 W 11 15
Sea 1.2 metre swell
wind very light NW
motor sailing at 240 magnetic

Unfortunately, the pleasant sail we were enjoying the previous afternoon, did not endure and last night at 21:00 hours I had to put in a double reef, as Aries was struggling to steer in the big seas and increasing wind. This morning we are now midway between Cape Spartel and Grand Canary and I really do not anticipate much change in the weather all the way to the Canaries. I expect the sea to remain mostly rough but hopefully I am wrong. Today, once again the returning light wind has made it necessary to run the engine but late in the afternoon I was able to stop it and set the boat to run on the main only, which seemed to suit Aries quite well. This is our fifth day at sea now and I am settling into a good working routine.

At 16:30 hours we are enjoying a beautiful sunny afternoon sail in a ten knot wind, the sea now much calmer. Grand Canary is now about 300 miles away.

Today this circumnavigation seems quite possible and my home-sickness is a thing of the past. I am starting to feel more confident in myself again since the Mediterranean experience.

A RETURN TO THE ATLANTIC

Sunday 13th March 2016
09:00 hours N 31 04 W 12 16
wind N 10 to 15 knots
sea 1 metre swell

We have covered 100 miles since 09:00 hours
yesterday and I have set Grace on a dead run, this is when
the wind is directly behind us and the spinnaker pole
holding out the genoa on the port side. An enjoyable sail
with the weather cloudy and warm. We are now in the
tropics and the days are so much warmer after February
in the Mediterranean. Beebee seems happy and relaxed
toileting twice a day without any problems. We saw a pod
of dolphins yesterday, much to her delight and this kept
her excited and alert for some time. She is enjoying her
dried food and seems to prefer sleeping in the cockpit at
night, albeit with her harness clipped on.

Monday 14th March 2016
N 29 33 W 14 11
wind calm sea flat
sunny clear sky

We are motoring slowly, making three knots over a
smooth sea under a cloudless sky, a really lovely
afternoon. Our run this noon was 200 miles in the last two
days, which I am quite satisfied with. Lanzarote island,
which is part of the Canaries, is visible on the beam and
we are now only 106 miles from Las Palmas in Grand

Canaria.

Tuesday 15th March 2016
wind light easterly 5 to 10 knots
sunny and warm swell slight

Grand Canaria is now 28 miles away, having motored the last 4 hours because of no wind, but nevertheless we have managed to cover 112 miles since 10:00 hours yesterday.

Now with imminent landfall, we should be at anchor before dark. I feel a great sense of satisfaction, since this is our first Atlantic run on the new mast and rigging since the dis-masting in the Mediterranean.

3

The Canaries

Tuesday 15th March 2016

It was a lovely warm sunny afternoon, when I dropped the anchor in Las Palmas anchorage at 16:00 hours, having sailed almost seven hundred miles from Gibraltar. I feel immensely content to be here, also quite satisfied with our performance with the new mast and equipment, having survived adversity and still being able to continue with our circumnavigation.

The following morning I was told to move Grace to the marina, as the anchorage was no longer in use for yachts. It has always been my preference to stay on anchor and row myself to the beach, but sadly this was no longer an option. Our stay in Grand Canary was as always, most enjoyable, this being my fourth visit on Grace. I soon made friends with other sailors in the marina, particularly Mark Lillingstone-Price, a former high ranking officer in the Gurkha regiment, who also had a wooden boat, albeit much larger at twenty metres. We could talk military matters together, as having been raised in the former British colony Rhodesia, I had spent years in the military as a territorial soldier and served there during the terrorist war in the seventies. I found him to be a very likeable man and also a true gentleman.

Time was also spent improving and tweaking the new rigging, including strengthening the fastenings to the mast at the spreader level. The engine mounts were checked, tightened and re-aligned because of previous problems. The alignment was now as perfect as I could get it and the engine ran with little or no vibration.

We took on 130 litres of diesel fuel, replenished our food stocks sufficient for an Atlantic crossing and also loaded on board four cases of cheap Spanish beer. I was now ready to go.

4

Leaving for the Atlantic crossing

22nd March 2016 Day 1
wind fresh NE 20 to 30 knots
boat speed 6 to 8 knots double reefed

We left on a very fresh north east wind making a fast get away, albeit with mixed feelings, sadness at leaving friends and the security of the marina. I suffered guilt at taking Beebee back to sea, after she had relished our long walks. I felt home-sick because I could no longer enjoy daily talks with Marilyn on skype. She telephoned me shortly before leaving to wish me "bon voyage".

The Atlantic crossing lay ahead and it was my intention to go south, almost to the Cape Verde Islands, before turning and heading west to Antigua. The first day at sea is always hard as things not properly stowed end up flying around the cabin and routines are not yet established. We seem to be neither at sea nor on land.

23rd March 2016 Day 2
wind light variable motoring at 3 knots
sea 1 metre swell
Run 101 miles

The wind died at 21:00 hours the previous night so I have been motoring all night, at a slow 3 knots in a slightly lumpy sea. Noon found us 101 miles from Grand Canaria and now we are sailing with the engine off on a very enjoyable beam wind, giving us 5 knots boat speed. At 22:00 hours the log records that we are double reefed and the wind is now blowing at 20 to 30 knots.

Earlier today Beebee had spotted a pod of dolphins racing down on us. This she always finds very exciting, resulting in her prancing around the deck barking with hysterical joy, definitely the high point of her day!

24th March 2016 Day 3
Run 107 miles
09:00 hours sea rough
double reefed wind 25 knots

The sails are still reefed from the night before and the Aries wind pilot has worked well, without requiring any attention through the night. Noon places us 208 miles from Grand Canaria, sailing with the wind on the quarter, at a steady 5 knots even though we are only carrying one third of our normal sail area. The sky is grey and overcast, but I am quite happy even though our motion is bouncy and uncomfortable, because we are making miles!

Beebee toileted at 17:00 hours and this was very difficult, with her skating across the deck, trying to find the perfect spot. Hopefully tomorrow might bring smoother seas with better weather but this section down to the Cape Verde islands is always rough, or so it has been the three previous times that Grace has sailed this route.

Friday 25th March 2016 Day 4
Run 105 mile
09:00 hours N 24 25 W 19 03
cloudy cool sea rough wind NE 25 knots

At 09:00 hours the sails are still reefed but we are making a steady 5 knots, which we had kept through the night and Aries steered the boat without any problems, requiring no attention from me at all. I had continually set the alarm for sixty minute intervals and on waking, would check the AIS for passing ships and of course stick my head out in case there were any fishing trawlers about, which never seem to show themselves on the AIS radar. I had often come upon them quite suddenly without any warning!

Noon finds us 313 miles from Grand Canaria which means we have made 105 miles since noon yesterday even though it had been rough overnight, so I am satisfied with our performance. The seas are still big with the occasional breaking sea knocking Grace off course but Aries in most cases manages to recover without my assistance. Beebee has had to spend all her time below decks in the cabin, but in this weather she does not seem to mind at all. We are now well established in our routines and becoming acclimatised to these continuously rough conditions.

Saturday 26th March 2016 Day 5
Run 116 miles
09:00 hours N 22 40 W 20 07
sunny cool sea rough 2 to 3 metre swells
N E wind 25 knots

During the previous night the sea became very rough and at times Aries failed to cope, which meant that I had to go out and re-set it. Seas were breaking on the boat on occasion, but nevertheless we managed to keep sailing at a reasonable speed. At 09:00 hours I record in the log that we have run 105 miles since noon yesterday which is was very good, when taking the sea conditions into account.

At noon I record that our run is 116 miles, which is the best since Gibraltar on the new mast. I write in the log of my pleasure in this figure, albeit being chased by half a gale. Nevertheless, the sea state is becoming very tiring, especially for Beebee who much prefers to stay in the cabin. It is difficult to toilet her, as she insists on finding the perfect spot on the deck, risking a soaking or worse. I managed only a few hours of very disturbed sleep having to continuously assist Aries in keeping on course and preventing the boat from gibing which was caused by wave action more so than by Aries. At 18:00 hours we are now 456 miles from Gran Canaria.

Sunday 27th March 2016 Day 6

Run 113 miles

sunny wind 25 to 30 knots

sea very rough

double reefed main tiny jib

09:00 hours N 20 50 W 20 39

We have now turned away from our Cape Verde heading, changing to a westerly course towards Antigua in the Caribbean. At 18:00 hours the log records us doing 6 knots in a very rough sea state, making life on board very uncomfortable and almost impossible to carry out any task including cooking. It leaves one with a buzzy head and a continuous feeling of slight nausea.

Once again our noon run is good at 113 miles.

Monday 28th March 2016 Day 7

Run 120 miles

cool cloudy wind 20 knots

sea rough 2 to 3 metre swell

heading 270 degrees magnetic

Throughout the previous night Grace steered quite successfully on our new heading at a speed of 6 knots. It is still rough but I suspect that this situation will not change until we are well into the trade wind belt.

Our noon to noon run shows as 120 miles on the GPS and this is a new record on this trip, all done on a double-reefed main and a tiny genoa. One can't compare the mileage on a crewed yacht with that of a solo boat, as a solo sailor has in effect no helmsman and will do anything to keep the wind pilot steering the yacht. This often includes choosing a heading which is not the best heading for mileage gain and also reefing when the preference would be not to, as the result would be a loss of speed but nevertheless having to do so to keep the wind pilot (Aries) steering a course somewhat in the chosen direction. This is particularly the case at three in the morning, when sleep is in short supply. Manually steering, that is taking over from Aries is really not an option because of fatigue or becoming over tired, which could be dangerous. There are many daily chores which need to be done, as well as meal preparation and of course the nights still require some watch keeping even on a solo crewed yacht.

Tuesday 29th March 2016 Day 8
Run 112
08:00 hours N 20 38 W 24 31
wind N 10 to 15 knots sea 1 metre swell
cloudy cool
heading 280 degrees magnetic at 5 knots

A quieter night with a few interruptions to reset Aries due to the falling wind. We are now heading deep into the Atlantic and I am pleased with our progress, even though it has been bumpy a lot of the time. My preference is to do 5 knots under full sail rather than 7 knots under a double reef.

Day by day I become happier with the new mast and smaller sail plan. We are making as good a speed, if not better than previously under the old mast and I know that Grace was definitely top heavy, so now it is my conviction that Ted, the original builder had fitted the wrong mast to this boat. It is just a pity though, that it has taken me sixteen years and five Atlantic crossings and one dis-masting to discover this!

Beebee is in a very happy mood today, quick to finish her breakfast and a very rapid visit to the toilet, which makes a refreshing change. Antigua is now 2,086 miles away and I hope to be there in about twenty days.

Wednesday 30th March Day 9
Run 135 miles
09:00 hours N 20 19 W 27 08
wind gusty 15 knots sea 1 metre swell
overcast cool

Our noon to noon run today is the amazing all-time record for Grace of 135 miles and we are now less than 2,000 miles, 1,934 to be exact, to Antigua. We enjoyed a superb sail all yesterday afternoon and through the night, a perfect wind at 15 knots on a flat sea. All night I constantly heard the 7 knots rumble from the propeller which is caused by the propeller rotating when the boat speed reaches 7 knots, giving out a smooth rumbling noise when it does, which is music in my ears.

Unfortunately, the short respite from strong winds is quickly over and we find ourselves once again double reefed at 17:00 hours on a rising sea, with the wind back to 25 knots.

Thursday 31st March 2016 Day 10

Run 110 miles

wind E 25 to 30 knots sea 3 metre swell

overcast and squally heading 265 mag.

09:30 hour double reefed main no jib

A difficult night for me as Aries struggled to steer in the very squally weather and big seas resulting in lost sleep. At 09:30 hours we have already done 100 miles, which I find quite amazing as she drifted whilst I slept for a few hours. I recorded in the log that "*last night was not a good night and today is no better.*"

I have already gained seven days on the previous crossing time that I did in 2012. I can tell this by looking at my original 2012 chart which I am re-using. I never erase old plots, as to me this is a historical record worth keeping. That was Beebee's first crossing with me to the West Indies and back to Kefalonia, showing me that she was a great boat dog!

Noon N 20 03 W 29 23

Our run for the previous twenty four hours is a very respectable 110 miles, which makes Antigua now 1,860 miles so we have sailed from Grand Canaria a total of 1,027 miles.

Friday 1st April 2016 Day 11
Run 110 miles
noon N 19 59 W 31 16
sea rough wind 20 to 30 knots
grey sky and cold

Another hard, cold night with very squally conditions, big seas, making self-steering difficult and sleep hard to find. It is at these times, that sailing is really not at all enjoyable. We are continuously being bashed about, always tensing up, waiting for a breaking sea to knock us off course. This resulting in having to put on oilskins and a harness and go on deck to re-set Aries. It is hard to find truly relaxing deep sleep. No sooner falling asleep, when the boat is thrown about and I find myself on the bottom end of my bunk.

We have nevertheless covered 110 miles again but I am still struggling to get our position below the twentieth parallel, where around 18 degrees we should find the north east trade winds. I could turn south by changing tack, but this would be even more inefficient than remaining on this tack, which definitely gives us better mileage.

Saturday 2nd April 2016 Day 12
Run 121 miles
Noon N 19 58 W 33 29
Antigua 1,621 miles
sea 2 to 3 metre swell
wind E 20 to 30 knots squally overcast

We have had four days now of heavy weather and I write in the log that I really could do with a break. It is really my own fault because of my reluctance to turn on a more southerly heading, it being my preference to gain mileage, in spite of taking the occasional wave on board.

However, another 121 miles is really appreciated and now we are 1,621 miles from Antigua.

Beebee, like myself, is in the doldrums caused by our bouncy, cold and wet environment and for her having to go on the deck to relieve herself is not easy and for me having to re-set Aries, risking a soaking is a constant hazard.

Sunday 3rd April 2016 Day 13 Hove-to
wind 30+ knots to gale force sea rough 5 metre swell

The wind from mid-morning started to increase dramatically and we were soon treble reefed and by noon, feeling tired and weary from sleep deprivation, I set the boat to heave-to in the occasionally breaking seas that were foaming and hissing down on to Grace from a great height. She, as always, would rise up buoyantly to let the main bulk of the wave flow harmlessly under us, repeating this sequence a hundred times. This is far too rough to put Beebee on the deck and if she cannot wait, and has to go in the cabin, then so be it, I will not mind cleaning up, as the risk of losing her is too great! I have no choice but to just wait out this gale, try to catch up on sleep or at the very least, just try to rest.

It is not easy to relax in this situation and I would be lying if I said that I was not worried. My trust in Grace is very strong, she is a well-built boat and has ridden out numerous gales with me in the past, but nevertheless a small breakage could expose a weakness in the boat not previously visible, causing knock-ons which could become very serious. It is impossible to forget that here we are in a hostile, alien environment, which we are not made for. We are very far from land or any help, totally on our own, relying solely on our own wits and luck for keeping us safe. Nevertheless, it is not healthy to dwell on "what ifs" but try to trust in the boat, in oneself and even though I am not religious by most definitions, I do believe in a creator or supreme being and so I do also put my trust in God, or as some would say, a higher power. Having another crew member on board would of course make this situation far easier for the simple reason that mutual discussions are so helpful in reducing the magnitude of problems and the reassurance from having another human being close by is so comforting, whilst being solo means having to dig a bit deeper in ones soul to find the assurances and comfort which is needed in hard times.

Monday 4th April 2016 Day 14
Run 20 miles
Noon N 19 38 W 35 46
wind E 15 knots
sea 3 to 4 metre swell rough
overcast and squally

After heaving to all night in the gale, I am now able to set Grace sailing again in the abating winds and seas, though still treble reefed. Our overnight drift on course was 20 miles and we also drifted south 22 miles, keeping us south of the twentieth parallel. At 17:00 hours I noted in the log that Aries was steering well in the calming seas and falling wind. We have sailed now 1,491 miles and now approaching half way to Antigua.

Tuesday 5th April 201 Day 15
Run 105 miles
08:00 hours N 18 43 W 36 50
Total run 1,485 miles
wind E NE 10 to 15 knots
squally morning grey some rain

Noon finds us becalmed between squalls as the weather is still very unsettled, forcing me to start the engine. I have set the boat to steer 250 magnetic which is south of the heading to Antigua and by so doing helps us to find the trade winds, which should take us out of this weather system.

The afternoon has cleared up considerably with a much lighter swell, the sun is now blessing us with its presence and the wind has also obligingly now dropped to a reasonable ten knots allowing me to set Grace on a course of 250 magnetic.

5

1974 Life in Rhodesia

A question as to why would someone want to go sailing on the ocean would not be out of place at this time and I must confess that I have frequently asked myself this. With me it all started, when as a young married man of just one year having settled into a new job with the Salisbury City Engineers Department in Rhodesia and paying off our mortgage. My wife Penny and I had been married for two years and we were thinking of starting a family. After having exciting work with contractors in Botswana and Malawi, I was now becoming increasingly bored with my new low pressure job as a municipal engineer in the roads and storm water development department.

I was twenty five years old and had spent all of my adult working life in the bush working for contractors building new roads and towns in previously undeveloped areas. My previous job had been an eighteen months contract on the Selibe Phikwe mine development project in Botswana, a multimillion dollar project turning the undeveloped desert into a mining project. This work I found exciting and creative and as a junior engineer I had been given huge responsibility, which came at the right time in my life, giving me the confidence that I had been lacking previously. It was a hot and balmy afternoon when work had slowed down to a mundane pace, that a fellow employee walked into the engineer's office, with whom I shared with two other engineers, and began to talk of building a sea going sailboat in the new medium of ferro-cement. This seemed at the time an easy and inexpensive way to build to build an oceangoing boat.

I had recently read a book written by Eric Hiscock called "Beyond The West Horizon" about a husband and wife team who sail their 28 foot wooden yacht around the world. I found this concept to be totally captivating, exciting and adventurous. Little did I know that the seeds had been sown in my sub-conscious mind and I would one day be doing precisely that but at this time the simple idea of owning a boat was enough. This chap continued in his conversation and as it turned out, he already owned plans and drawings for the building of a 32 foot ferro-cement yacht, which he was quite happy for me to copy.

In no time at all I had copied the drawings and convinced Penny that building a boat would be a way of getting money out of Rhodesia which now had severe restrictions on taking money out. I had Penny's agreement on the condition that we would start a family and in due course Penny became pregnant.

At this time the terrorist war situation was deteriorating and so the military commitment that all young Rhodesians had was becoming more and more lengthy. We were all in the territorial army and had to frequently leave our jobs and families and join our battalions on the border to prevent the incursion of terrorists who were attacking the white farmers on the rural farms and trying to overthrow the white government by force.

Penny and I both felt that the inevitable would take place, resulting in us having to leave the country of our birth. I might add that these attacks were not only restricted to farmers but the rural blacks were also being attacked. If the terrorists thought that they were not supporting their cause or for that matter any number of other reasons, so much so that the rural tribesman suffered huge loss of life, far in excess of the killings of whites.

A ferro cement boat requires firstly to build a boat shaped bird cage using steel rods which are then covered in eight layers of fine chicken wire mesh. This "armature" as it is called is then plastered in a strong sand-cement mixture, thus forming a ferro cement hull, which is only 25 millimetres thick, but due to the high metal reinforcing content in the skin, is immensely strong and absolutely waterproof. In this way a boat hull is formed, ready for painting and fitting out. Many of these ferro cement boats have circumnavigated the world very successfully.

On the 1st December 1974 the boat was plastered by a team made up of two professional plasterers and three fellow boat builders, all building ferro cement boats. I had previously helped plaster their boats, thus learning the process and they returned the favour. This job was done in a day and the following lunchtime Fiona, my daughter was born in Princess Margaret Hospital in

Salisbury.

Both Penny and I were exhausted at the end of the day, but for different reasons, and needless to say, I was a proud father.

6

1977 Leaving Rhodesia

Three years later, after selling our house, Penny, Fiona and I left for South Africa with my brother Doug, who had helped build the boat, now named Just So. Rudyard Kipling's Just So stories were a favourite of mine and my siblings, which were read to us by our mother, when we were young children. Doug was not as besotted as I was about sailing on the ocean, but like Penny and I, he had also decided to leave Rhodesia, so he had put time and money into the construction of the boat. Many similar boats were being moved out of the country for the same reasons by other Rhodesians.

Our little family and Doug boarded the train in Salisbury and shared a compartment all the way to Durban in South Africa, after changing trains once in Johannesburg. We also had with us our German Shephard dog, who I had trained with a dog training club almost to obedience champion standard. He was loved by all and was such a loyal beautiful animal who adored our little daughter Fiona, she would screech with laughter whenever he licked her face. Caesar was his name and one strange feature about his character was whenever I was called up to join my battalion in the army for the usual six week stint, he would take command at home letting no one on to our gated property unless accompanied by Penny, my wife. This would include friends and relatives who he knew well, but once I returned from my military commitment he would revert to his old happy self, and become everyone's friend again!

The boat had left Salisbury a week before on the back of a low-loader truck and would be transported to a boat yard in Durban.

On our arrival, our first task was to find somewhere to live and so we quickly found an apartment quite close to the boat yard. I took up employment with the Durban City Engineers department doing similar work to what I had being doing in Salisbury. Doug had his own place nearer town and so we all settled into a new life which included working weekends on Just So, doing the final fitting out and installing the engine and not least of all, learning to sail and acquiring the necessary experience and papers to captain a yacht off-shore. These were the requirements of the Durban port authority.

Nearly two years later Just So which had started life 800 miles away in land locked Rhodesia, was finally ready to begin her travels on the ocean. We planned to sail to Cape town but the big, much talked about problem was Caesar our dog, what to do with him. Was it cruel to take such a large animal on a small boat across the ocean? He adored all of us but particularly me, as we had trained together since he was a puppy and now he was over six years old. Finally the decision was taken to re-home him and a delightful family were very happy to have him, but nevertheless, I was an emotional wreck for days after this and it was only that we had put so much into Just So, made me proceed with our original intentions and not stay on in Durban with the engineers department and keep our beloved Caesar.

Doug and I set sail for Cape town, accompanied by two friends. Penny and Fiona were to join us on our arrival there. Just So had undergone extensive sea trials in Durban and some work which had been done in Rhodesia, had to be changed due to our inexperience.

Our sail to Cape Town was to say the least, a hard, traumatic sea-sickness experience. Our crew left us at the first opportunity, which was our stop in East London, so Doug and I carried on our own down the South African coast, considered to be one of the most dangerous in the world, due to frequent gales in conjunction with strong currents. At this time there were no GPS or AIS systems, internet or even accurate weather forecasting. Not that we would have had any of these if they had been available, as our budget would not stretch that far. Furthermore, our money was needed to get us to the Caribbean, our eventual destination. We also had no communication radio on board, so if in distress we would have had a problem. Despite the sea sickness, one of us had to steer the boat day and night.

During the next two weeks, we suffered at least two strong gales and at one stage, were even blown back up the coast twenty miles! We arrived in Cape town exhausted, very thin, but much more experienced than when we left Durban. My dear brother Doug never complained during the trip but said to me on our arrival in Cape town *"If I ever get back on a boat again, you had better shoot me because it will only be because I have gone stark, staring mad!"*

Doug left me at the yacht club gate with only a small bag containing all his worldly possessions. We shook hands and said our farewells and he walked off down the road towards the city where he would catch a train to Pretoria. He was to stay with our married sister Audrey and hopefully get work. I felt very sad at his leaving, because we had been through so much together, not just the trip down the coast but also the building of Just So in Rhodesia. We had always been very close as friends, I suppose because he was only one year older than I and all through our school days we would stand by one another and be known as the Campbell brothers. I knew that I would miss him terribly.

Penny, Fiona and I remained in Cape Town for another year and I was able to secure work with a large civil engineering contractor. Following this, we left Cape Town, this time we were accompanied by Conny, my youngest sister, and her boyfriend Brian. We successfully sailed Just So via St Helena to Brazil where Conny and Brian left us to explore South America. Penny, Fiona and I continued on to the West Indies exploring the island chain, picking up work wherever possible and enjoying the carefree island life.

We carried on through the Bahamas eventually ending our voyage in Florida, where Just So was sold, two years after leaving Cape Town.

We returned to Durban where Penny, Doug and I started a small but quite successful furniture factory. My son Neil was born nine months after our return to South Africa.

Five years later Penny, Fiona, Neil and I left South Africa on our new 38 foot fibre-glass yacht which we had named Tumbler, heading once again for the West Indies. Our intention was to sell this boat in Florida and then take up residence in America. Doug stayed on in Durban as manager for the new owners of the factory.

In due course Tumbler was sold in Florida and after a year we moved to North Carolina where we lived and worked for another two years. Sadly, we missed our family and so once again we moved, this time to England where both my sisters lived as well as my mother and stepfather.

England was more suitable for our family and of course Fiona and Neil had their grandparents, aunts and cousins. Both children received excellent education, finally earning degrees from Cardiff University. Sadly, as often happens in modern life, Penny and I drifted apart and became divorced in 1997.

BEYOND THE SUNSET

7

Successful crossing

Wednesday 6th April 2016 Day 17
08:00 hours N 17 57 W 38 12
wind E NE 10 knots sea 2 m swell
grey overcast occasional rain squalls
heading 250 magnetic

At noon the wind has now dropped to a flat calm and so we are motoring on a course direct for Antigua which is 271 magnetic. I had started the engine at 08:00 and we are now 1,339 miles from Antigua. Our run for the last twenty four hours is 95 miles which is quite OK.

Running the engine at 1,200 rpm is giving us a speed of about 5 knots but I am not always happy with doing so as it spoils the peace and solitude of sailing which is one of the reasons I like open ocean. During the afternoon the sky cleared and we began to enjoy a beautiful sunny day with no more squalls and the sea is becoming calmer. The sky is clear and a beautiful blue.

We were visited by a pod of dolphins who played in our bow wave for at least twenty minutes much to Beebee's delight, who ran around the deck in hysterical excitement. Flying fish were now quite abundant, jumping out of the waves and gliding at times for fifty yards or more before splashing back into the sea. Sadly, these creatures, sometimes up to ten centimetres in length, would land on the deck at night and I would find them dead in the morning. There is definitely more of a Caribbean feeling in this part of the ocean.

I have been reading Ellen McArthur's book, which I am enjoying immensely. She is an amazing sailor, so inspiring and it seems we share the same love and passion for our boats, which at times others find difficult to understand. One of my reasons for sailing the ocean is the passion I hold for my boat, the sea I am not so enamoured with. To me it is a necessary requirement to enable me to enjoy my boat, particularly before the onset of old age and lost opportunity. People have been known to say that I am trying to prove something but I disagree, it is just that life's pleasures must be enjoyed now, with no time wasted because life is like money, which means it cannot be taken with you when you die!

Friday 8th April 2016 Day 18
Run 118 mile
08:00 hours N 15 52 W 42 00
wind E 10-15 knots
sea 1-2 metre swell
overcast with showers

The wind picked up overnight and we managed to maintain a steady sail on 270 magnetic at 5 knots. The improving wind this morning has pushed up the speed now to 6 knots plus, so with the advancing of the time today (I have to re-set the clocks today) this giving us an extra hour, which makes our run twenty five hours, so giving me a few extra miles in our days run and so our noon to noon run was now 118 miles.

Unfortunately, nothing lasts and by 19:00 hours we are once again back to three reefs and a tiny jib, in strong squally winds with sweeping cold rain. So much for Caribbean conditions!

Monday 11th April 2016 Day 19
Run 90 miles
08:00 hours N 16 25 W 47 04
wind falling E 10-15 sea 2 metre
clear and sunny

Until today the weather has not improved, with rainy squalls and rough seas since the 8 of April but today is promising a change from previous weeks. Noon found us motoring in calm conditions, with Ray (electric auto pilot) steering as the wind is far too light for Aries.

I kept myself busy today by doing some much needed jobs which included tightening the steering, replacing the sail slides in the mainsail which had been breaking at a steady rate because the Chinese company who had supplied the sail had used inferior plastic slides and spaced them too far apart. This was in spite of ordering a sail to be heavy duty, as it was to be used for a circumnavigation. This was the specification that I gave at the time I placed the order, and here I am, in the middle of the ocean trying to make metal slides from bits of brass with a file and a hacksaw!

Tuesday 12th April 2016 Day 22
Run 93 miles
08:00 hours N 16 14 W 48 40
Antigua 737 miles
wind E 10-15 knots sea 1-2 metre
sunny heading 300 magnetic

Aries is steering so much better since the rudder cables were tightened, I should have done it before! I changed more broken sail slides today with my homemade metal ones and also using some quality nylon slides which I had to modify, from my previous mainsail. Very pleased with myself and my hand sewing. We could now be in the Caribbean trade wind system and it has become much warmer than it has been in the last few weeks.

Wednesday 13th April 2016 Day 23
Run 105 miles
08:00 Hours N 16 03 W 50 37
Antigua 632 miles
wind E 10-15 knots sea 1 metre
sunny occasional squalls

Enjoyed a perfect sail all yesterday and through the night in light winds and clear skies under full sail plan, running with the jib poled out on a port tack. It is

marvellous to be sailing again under a starry velvet sky
with a wonderful clarity in the air giving us a beautiful
spread of the milky way, which sadly we haven't seen
enough of this trip. The evening is warm and Grace is
moving along without fuss, just covering miles, and the
sails were so perfect in their shape, without a flutter at all,
as if they had been sculptured from metal. This sort of
sailing is what ocean passage making is all about! We have
had no ship sightings since a few days out of Grand
Canaria and this makes catching up on sleep a lot easier.
Trying to sleep in the day is always difficult, even though it
is definitely the safest option.

We are still nine days ahead of our previous
crossing time so all in all Grace is doing well, maintaining
our daily average of 100 miles a day, which compared to
modern boats is not good but then she is almost fifty years
old and is a heavy design, built in no way as a race boat.

Tuesday19th April 2016 Day 29
Run 57 miles
08:00 hours N 16 26 W 59 11
Antigua 152 miles
wind E very light warm a few clouds
sea little swell

We have 152 miles to go and the wind is, as it has
been for the last five days, very light. Our mileages have
been low, averaging about 70-80 miles a day and now we
are low on fuel, so I need to be very frugal with running

the engine to guarantee a safe passage into Antigua, ensuring enough fuel for the last 50 miles. It would be easy to be swept past the island if there was no wind as the current runs at up to two knots between the islands. I had really hoped to make a landfall tomorrow but if these conditions persist it might be difficult to make a daylight arrival and night arrivals are too risky for single-handed sailors. At 16:00 hours we are still motoring at slow speed, hoping for wind.

20th April 2016 Day 30
07:30 hours N 16 38 W 60 59
Antigua 51 miles
wind N E 10-15 overcast rain showers
sea 1 metre swell

Eventually the wind picked up at 23:00 hours last night, much to my relief, allowing us to make four knots through the night, with Aries steering without fault. This now makes a daylight landfall very possible!

Now we are motor-sailing at six knots and desperately hoping that the wind holds. Excitement is building and Guadeloupe Island is visible on the port beam, about thirty miles away. At noon I record in the logbook that this would be my last entry before Antigua and for this Atlantic crossing, having sailed 2,894 miles from Gran Canaria and over 4,500 miles from Kefalonia.

We are now less than thirty miles from English Harbour, our chosen destination and the islands profile is becoming visible against the clouds directly ahead.

At 14:00 hours local time we approached the island in light, warm tropical rain, the wind a steady ten knots and Grace moving well under full sail with the engine running at 1,200 rpm. The smell of the damp tropical island is so intoxicating, different compared to the smells we had over the last month. I find it emotionally overwhelming, as we entered English Harbour, seeing the familiar gun batteries from Nelson's time and the yachts anchored at Nelson's dockyard. Tears of joy ran down my face as we quietly motored past anchored yachts into the inner anchorage. Grace had been to Antigua three times previously and so we headed for the anchorage we had used before, which was back in the inner harbour. I dropped the anchor, switched off the engine and we quietly lay in the little anchorage, very still and only the birds and island life to be heard, surrounded by smells and life which we had not experienced for weeks. I felt immensely proud, relieved and full of joy, walking on clouds and so proud of Grace who had worked tirelessly, faithfully and so reliably to get us here.

Beebee is all over the deck, very impatient for me to launch the dinghy so as to get ashore and explore. She fully understood this complete change to our circumstances.

After a very pleasant week in Nelsons dockyard and long walks with Beebee to the beaches, we set off once again bound for the neighbouring island of St Martin, a day sail away and on arrival we anchored off the French end of the island in Marigot Harbour. Shortly after dropping the anchor, my old friends from the previous crossing in 2011 came alongside in their dinghy. Their names are Vasil and Inga, both Germain sailors who are also in the process of doing a circumnavigation but now working in St Martin to stock up the coffers. They are dear friends of mine. Inga is younger than Vasil who is in his forties. Both are very competent people and there is no trade that Vasil can't do to a high standard, forever kind and helpful. Inga is beautiful and a little shy but a talented cartoonist with a wicked sense of humour. Both love their 34 foot boat and make a wonderful loving, sailing partnership. I spent most nights on board their boat drinking rum with them and other sailors who would drop by. This camaraderie is what makes life on the ocean so pleasant and rewarding.

Beebee in the West Indies again

I left after a week, with Vasil making sure I lacked for nothing and forever helpful with my boat problems. We said our farewells and I sailed for St John in the American Virgin Islands where my daughter and her American husband lived with their two little girls, Georgia and Rae. They have a house on the hill overlooking Fish Bay on the south of the island. A day and a night sail brought me into Fish Bay, having to feel my way past the reef which guarded the entrance to the bay. Definitely a daylight entry only, thus making it unpopular with local yachtsmen and except for two little fishing boats, we have this beautiful bay surrounded by hills, all to ourselves.

8

The time in St John

The first thing I did after our arrival, was to set a second anchor which in effect became a mooring so that even though the bay was perfectly protected, I could leave Grace for long periods without worrying. Amongst the mangroves I spotted a small beach where I could land and safely leave the dinghy.

I enjoyed a wonderful reunion with my daughter Fiona, her husband Justin, and my two granddaughters Georgia and Rae, aged four and two years old. Over the next three months in St John, I would help Justin on his boat, which was having the engines re-built and other extensive refurbishment work. It was a power catamaran, an ex-charter boat about 45 feet long and he was hoping to charter it once all the work was completed. Justin and I also worked on the house doing maintenance and improvements. Their house was situated about two hundred yards up the hill, a very easy walk from the boat and overlooked the bay so that my arrival had been watched by the family.

Beebee and I would spend every evening with the family and after dinner we would walk down through the mangroves, along the marked path to our little beach and row back to the boat. I would enjoy a cup of coffee in the cockpit, taking in the beautiful surroundings, listening to the crickets and wildlife in the mangroves, before falling into my bunk.

During this time Neil my son, who is a school teacher in the UK. was able to come to the island and stay with Fiona and Justin for a ten days holiday. This was really so rewarding to have both my children and grandchildren all together. Neil and I did a four days sail to Norman Island taking in Jost van Dyke and other islands on the way. We stayed a night in Great Harbour on Jost van Dyke and enjoyed a meal at Foxy's beach bar, one of the world's most famous beach bars. A wooden boat race is held here annually in May and in 2007 Fiona, Justin and I sailed Grace here from Grand Canaria across the Atlantic to take part in this popular regatta. It is known as one of the best party weekends in the Virgin Islands and the bay is full with scores of visiting boats both private and charter during the race weekend. My time with Neil was special and I will remember it as one of our best.

All too soon it was time to leave for Panama as the hurricane season was now with us and I needed to get below the tenth parallel in order to leave the hurricane belt before August, the most dangerous time of the hurricane season.

9

Voyage to Panama

Tuesday 2nd August 2016 Day 1

16:00 hours

wind N E 15 knots

sea 1 metre swell

sunny clear sky

We left Fish Bay at 10:00 hours and motored around to Cruz Bay where I anchored Grace so as to clear customs and immigration. After topping up our water and fuel tanks at the fuel station we sailed out of the beautiful Cruz Bay, heading past Christmas cove on the island of Great St James and then pointed Grace in the direction of Panama, heading out into the Caribbean Sea.

I had said my sad farewells to the family after enjoying our last breakfast together on the island and my granddaughters gave Beebee and I big hugs. Leaving was hard, as I had really got to know the little girls, so precious, it would be a long while before I would see them again.

Wednesday 3rd August 2016 Day 2
08:00 hours N 17 35 W 65 38
wind 15 knots E sea slight
sunny and hot
heading 240 magnetic

At noon we are 947 miles from Christobal with the wind now up to 15 to 20 knots and a rising sea. The day is very hot and humid but I am pleased that we are making over five knots under a full suite of sails. Grace is pushing on nicely with a barnacle free hull, because I had scraped off all the growth that had accumulated during our stay in Fish Bay. I did this by diving under the boat using a mask and snorkel.

My first night at sea is a bit squally, so I could not sleep well, also having to keep an eye open for marine traffic between the islands. It always takes a couple of days to return to our routines.

Thursday 4th August 2016 Day 3
Run 101 miles
wind 15 to 20 E sea moderate
mixed sun and cloud

I had to take in two reefs at midnight as the wind had picked up to 25 knots, bringing with it rough seas. At regular intervals a ship would appear, leaving me no choice but to cat nap for short spells. Nevertheless, Aries worked well and so far no problems, touch wood!

We are now 840 miles from Christobal, at the entrance to the Panama Canal.

Friday 5th August 2016 Day 4
Run 94 miles
08:00 hours N 15 20 W 68 18
wind E squally 20 to 30 knots sea rough
double reefed heading 220 magnetic

During the previous night the wind picked up, gusting to 30 knots, so I was forced to change our heading to 220 magnetic to keep Aries working. Our run at noon (in the direction of Panama) was only 92 miles, mainly due to our heading and the rough weather and seas. At 16:00 hours the wind eased noticeably, so I reset Grace on a direct run downwind on full main and genoa. This took time to get Aries and Grace to work in harmony on an improved heading of 250 magnetic.

An entry in the log shows my feeling of homesickness where I write "*it seems my three months at anchor in Fish bay is already a distant memory. It was an enjoyable stay and the longest I have lived at anchor in the same place. A quiet and beautiful bay, all to myself but close to Fiona and the family for our daily visits.*"

Saturday 6th August 2016 Day 5
Run 110 miles
08:00 hours N 14 29 W 69 52
wind 15-20 knots warm and sunny
steering 250 magnetic on dead run

Aries steered well through the night maintaining a steady speed on a good course. Yesterday I spoke to two ships which passed very close to us, less than two miles away and they confirmed that my AIS system was working well. This equipment will alert shipping of my presence, thus it is a wonderful safety feature to have on board a single handed yacht!

At noon I write in the log that although our run is much improved, I should be getting better speeds with these steady 15-20 knot winds. We have now left the hurricane belt which means no more hurricane worries. Currently we are enjoying a broad reach on full main and jib on a heading of 250 magnetic, making a satisfying 6 knots. This is the best sail since leaving Fish Bay, with no more squalls and a steady wind. Grace is driving ahead eagerly and life is near perfection!

Sunday 7th August 2016 Day 6
Run 124 miles
08:00 hours N 13 35 W 71 41
Panama 546 miles
wind 15-20 E sea 2 metre swell rough

I had to reef again at midnight after the boat gibed in a 20-30 knot wind but suffered no damage, due to the preventer catching the mainsail in a timely fashion. (A gibe is when the wind gets behind the main and violently throws it across the boat to the other side, often causing great damage to the sails and other equipment.) At noon I recorded in the log, a very good run of 124 miles and even though we were sailing only on main and staysail, our boat speed was at times was exceeding six knots.

As twilight approached at 19:00 hours, I went on to the bow and enjoyed the huge bow wave that Grace was throwing out to lea. She looked so beautiful with all the sails, now a golden red colour, drawing so dramatically and I realised that we were sailing at 7 knots, over the bronze sea in the last minutes of the fading daylight. I let out an uncontrolled shout of joy!

Monday 8th August 2016 Day 7
Run 110 miles
N 12 19 W 73 48
wind 20-30 knots sea rough overcast
Panama 414 miles

At 02:00 hours I once again had to put in two reefs as the wind had been picking up all morning but by noon I set the sails in a hove-to mode as Aries could no longer steer the boat in the increasing wind. Heaving to causes the boat to drift to lea, thus creating a slick which absorbs the waves, mostly on the bow. This requires a treble reefed main and a small staysail which is set backed against the wind.

Tuesday 9th August 2016 Day 8
N 12 05 W 74 00
wind 35-40 knots sea very rough overcast

All day the wind has remained gale force and the seas have become very rough and breaking, possibly 6-8 metres in height. At times like this life is very miserable and there is little that can be done except wait it out. It is quite impossible to take Beebee on deck to toilet, also to do anything like making a cup of tea runs the risk of scalding by a flying cup of water. The bunk is wet and the hatches and portholes are dripping with sea water from waves which frequently wash over the deck. It is hot and humid in the cabin and sleep is almost impossible. I write in the log *"Thank the Lord for plenty of sea room,"* that is no land in the proximity, as Grace can survive well in deep water but coastlines and shallow water are deadly to her in storm conditions! All sailors are very fearful of a lea shore which is when the wind and the waves are driving a vessel on towards a coastline.

Wednesday 10th August 2016 Day 9

08:00 hours N 11 47 W 74 11

wind 20-25 E sea rough

We are now sailing again as the wind has dropped in the early hours of the morning. The last forty eight hours has been very difficult with these big seas and gale force winds, so unusual for the Caribbean summer, unless we had been caught by a tropical storm and this is their breeding ground after all!

At noon, the wind has quickly dropped and the sea is now back to a one to two metre swell with the sun now very apparent. We are about twenty five miles from the Columbian coastline and closing due to a wind swing to east north east.

BEYOND THE SUNSET

Thursday 11th August 2016 Day 10
Panama 294 miles
08:00 hours N 11 26 W 75 28
wind 25-30 knots
sea rough 5 metre swell
mostly cloudy

We managed only eleven hours of sailing yesterday before having to heave to again in strong winds at 23:00 hours yesterday.

Today I am feeling low and exhausted caused by continuous sail handling yesterday and very little sleep overnight. I can't believe the bad weather that we have had to endure for the last three days. The wind has never stopped blowing since leaving St John, always in excess of twenty knots which is tiring for a solo sailor.

At noon I write in the log that we are now sailing again since 10:00 hours on the second reef, steering 289 magnetic, the wind is dropping and I am holding my breath that it does not pick up with nightfall.

Friday 12th August 2016 Day 11
Run 78 miles
08:00 hours N 11 17 W 76 45
wind 10 knots E sea 1 metre swell
sunny and clear heading 240 magnetic

The wind remained steady and light overnight which was such a refreshing change, allowing me to catch up on sleep and Aries very obligingly kept us on a good course all night without requiring any attention at all!

At around noon the wind dropped, so it became necessary to start the engine but I had difficulty in getting Ray, the electric auto-pilot, to steer the boat at first, but eventually managed to proceed at four knots.

Today we will have completed ten sailing days and originally I was sure that we would be in Panama by now, I do put this down to losing three days of travelling time due to storms.

Saturday 13th August 2016 Day 12
Run 57 miles
08:00 hours N 10 36 W 77 27
Christobal 166 miles
wind calm very hot sea slight
heading 244 magnetic motoring at 1,300 rpm

At noon we are still motoring over a long smooth swell but our run is not good at 57 miles, not surprising really, considering that from midnight until 08:00 hours we sailed at 1 to 2 knots, barely making steerage. I do not believe in running the engine whilst sleeping, so I rarely do this, therefore we only had these light winds for our overnight mileage.

Sunday 14th August 2016 Day 13
Run 52 miles
wind N E 10 knots slight swell
Panama 414 miles

As usual, we had very light winds overnight, too light to steer, so we drifted most of the time. I started the engine at 08:00 hours, we are now motoring at 250 magnetic. At noon we have sailed only 52 miles in twenty four hours, and still the wind has not returned.

At 13:00 hours disaster struck! The flexible coupling to the gearbox failed, so we immediately lost our transmission, rendering the engine useless, so we have no means of propulsion except for the wind. The transmission cannot be repaired without spare parts! This is very alarming because it means that I will have to enter Colon harbour under sail. After examination of the chart I see that this may not be a huge problem as the harbour behind the breakwater is very large, so as long as we have wind, we will be alright.

Monday 15th August 2016 Day 14
08:00 hours
becalmed wind 0 knots
overcast

We have been totally becalmed since yesterday, and experienced heavy thunder storms overnight, but still without any wind at all, so we are just drifting and waiting for better weather, I sorely miss the use of the engine! Our twenty four hours run is zero, but we had drifted two miles south.

Tuesday 16th August 2016 Day 15
18:00 hours N 10 02 W 78 42
wind very light sea large swell
warm and overcast
heading 228 magnetic

We are now sailing slowly south at two knots in a very fluky breeze which is continually changing direction. This same breeze kept me busy all night sailing in circles, and often going backwards towards St John. All this effort has really been a waste of time and sleep. I feel extremely frustrated at not having the use of the engine.

I took down the genoa and made some repairs to it and tried to keep my sanity by doing household chores. My appetite for reading books seems to have escaped me at the moment and my only therapy is to keep busy.

Wednesday 17th August 2016 Day 16
Christobal 65 miles
08:00 hours N 10 05 W 79 04
wind 10 E
sea rough short seas 3 metre swell

I fail to understand why the seas are so unsettled with these light wind conditions; maybe it is due to the sea becoming much shallower in this area as we approach the coast.

Noon found us once again becalmed and drifting. We were becalmed all yesterday until 20:00 hours, then a light east north east wind allowed us to keep steerage through the night, almost on a dead run, steering 260 magnetic. We are now being kept company by a steady flow of shipping every few hours. At 14:00 hours we lose the wind and drift again. I expect to see shore lights tonight as we are now fifty one miles from Christobal. The breeze picked up at 20:00 hours and we are once again able to make steerage.

Thursday 18th August 2016 Day 17
Run 65 miles

A steady breeze picked up late last night and kept us sailing through the night on a broad reach. I was shocked and horrified to see land on the beam at 02:00 hours about two miles off-it seems we were much closer than I thought. This comes of sailing blindly in the dark without proper charts! I only had one that covered the whole of the Caribbean Sea which was a small scale, showing no detail. Shortly after this we passed very close to a fish farm, fortunately it was well lit, as I was snatching the odd half hour to sleep during the night.

At 09:00 hours the Cristobal breakwater came into view, a very welcome sight directly in front of us. This sail was quite fortuitous as on our approach to land the perfect wind had appeared, to give me control of Grace all the way to the breakwater. Without this breeze I could have found myself in a dangerous situation drifting on to rocks or in the path of a ship and having no way of powering to safety. I passed through the entrance to the channel, still being blessed by the wind, immediately called the signal station, who directed me to anchor near the buoy Echo 4, which I did. The radio operator was very polite and professional, I was too tired to feel overjoyed at this landfall but nevertheless was quietly pleased to be lying at anchor in the harbour, watching a continuous stream of shipping coming in and out of the harbour, all waiting their clearance to transit the Panama canal. I feel proud of the sail we have accomplished, all under wind power and difficult winds at that.

The next two days was spent getting customs and immigration clearance. This proved quite difficult as the various offices were in different parts of town and also expensive as I had also to pay for a cruising permit and a visitor's visa all at a cost in excess of 300 dollars. There were also bribes to pay, so I am really not impressed with Christobal and Panama!

The sixteen day sail from St John turned out to be two days and three nights hove-to in winds over thirty knots. The seas were always rough, even when becalmed. Because of safety reasons I wouldn't run the engine at night (whilst sleeping) in calms resulting in us drifting for three nights. On the thirteenth day the failure of the transmission resulted in us having no engine for the rest of the trip which happened just before the four days calm, when we had no wind at all! So, the total result of storms, no wind and no engine made this trip seven days longer than it could have been.

Two days after our arrival I decided to move Grace over to Shelter Bay marina under sail power for a haul out to anti-foul the bottom in preparation for the long Pacific crossing.

Once entering the shipping channel sailing now in the falling light wind I receive on the VHF radio "*Grace, Grace this is traffic control, you are entering the shipping channel be aware we have incoming traffic*" I replied, "*Port control, I am aware of my position and will proceed as fast I can out of the channel but I have an overheating engine so I am deliberately going slowly.*" (I dare not admit that I have no working engine as I would be instructed to take a tow possibly at a huge expense, this is Panama!) "*Grace, Grace I must advise you that movement in the harbour area under sail is prohibited, please proceed as quickly as you can out of the channel as we have imminent traffic arriving.*" I replied, "*Thank you for your understanding and I shall shortly leave the channel.*" Five minutes later I managed to exit the channel, heading now across the harbour, the remaining two miles to Shelter Bay in the now almost non-existent wind.

"*Grace, Grace this is Port control you are now entering the restricted area for anchoring ships which carry explosives and I must inform you that I have a ship New Horizon proceeding now to this anchorage, you will be*

*obstructing the passage of this vessel, please leave this
area immediately!"* F..... g hell! As if I have not got enough
problems! I now hear Port control informing this incoming
ship to proceed with caution as there is a very slow moving
yacht Grace in its path. New Horizon replied with irritation
*"We have Grace visible directly on our course and this is a
dangerous situation."* I looked behind and was shocked to
see, a quarter of a mile away, an extremely large bulk
carrier painted in bright orange heading directly for me!

At this stage a fourth party entered this VHF
conversation, a support pilot vessel stating that it was
prepared to tow Grace out of the path of New Horizon.
"Grace, Grace standby to take a tow." And almost
immediately a 40 foot pilot vessel was violently banging
alongside Grace. I shouted to the pilot of the vessel to
stand off to allow me to prepare my fenders. This he did
and I instead gave him my tow line and told him to
proceed as slowly as possible. At this stage New Horizon
was almost on top of us and because of this the captain of
the tow vessel accelerated at high speed in a panic,
breaking my tow line. I decided to ignore the intimidating
presence of New Horizon behind us and gave the towing
vessel another rope. This time he decided to pay attention
to my instructions and gently towed Grace to Shelter Bay
entrance where I dropped the anchor. He almost refused to
do this and insisted that he tow me into the marina. Under
no circumstance would I allow this inexperienced captain
to tow me in the confines of this marina which is crammed
with expensive yachts. In fairness to the man, his normal

duties would never have entailed the towing of fragile yachts. I lived in dread during the next few days, always anticipating the presentation of a large towing bill from the port authority which I am pleased to say never did appear!

After this very stressful day my nerves were shredded so I decided to row Beebee any myself to Shelter Bay marina bar, where I spoilt myself with a stiff drink! I met Ollie, Donna and Daniel Moser a lovely South African family from the yacht Kaya Margarita. Ollie offered to tow me into the marina the following morning. Over the next few days we became close friends and I enjoyed the family's company enormously.

During our stay at Shelter Bay whist Grace was being hauled and painted, I made many new friends amongst the international sailing community, most of whom were also planning a Pacific transit.

Beebee of course loved the freedom of running around the boat yard and club during the haul out. The friendly, helpful staff all added to a pleasant stay in Shelter Bay and I managed to get the part for the transmission which arrived in five days after ordering from England. This I fitted in two hours and had the transmission working again shortly before relaunching and motoring back to Christobal, where I anchored off the yacht club. This club offered free use of its facilities and for a small charge I could leave the dinghy in security at the club.

From this cheaper anchorage I was able to organise the canal transit, pay the canal company the fee

and the refundable deposit. Unfortunately Shelter Bay was
a little out of budget for a longer stay.

The refundable deposit of 800 dollars would be
forfeited if I were to break down and not do the transit in
the allocated time, or fail to maintain a minimum speed of
five knots.

On the morning of eighth of September I returned
to Shelter Bay to pick up my four crew members who were
to act as line handlers, a requirement by the canal
company. They were Malcolm Williams, younger than me
and from the Midlands in England who was a very
experienced delivery captain. Mike, an Australian in his
fifties, a no nonsense man also very capable, waiting to
also do the transit, and was coming along for the
experience. A nice guy who got stuck in with any chore,
would make sandwiches and pass around drinks etcetera
without being asked. He came on board with a huge
hamper of food and drinks, to make sure everyone would
have a good time. Then there was Pierre, a French guy, a
very competent ocean racer with a terrific sense of
humour. I must give Pierre full marks for pulling together
my line handlers, doing this in Shelter Bay and
telephoning me frequently to tell me how the recruitment
process was proceeding. His efforts really helped me
enormously as I had a huge amount of things to organise
as well as looking after the comforts of the crew for the
overnight trip on Grace. Pierre also arranged the Shelter
Bay kitchen to provide the evening meal for the crew and
the Panamanian pilot who would be with us for the first

day.

The only lady on board was a Californian called Nicole who was about forty years old, not very experienced but nevertheless good company who came along to add to her holiday experience. I will add here, that all the line handlers were voluntary and had come along purely for the experience and fun of it. Some yachts in the past have been obliged to pay for Panamanian line handlers to do the transit and this can work out to be quite expensive as the return taxi journey from the Pacific side must also be paid for.

The line handlers work was to control the boat, using long lines as the water flowed in and out of the locks, one end of each rope being held on Grace and the other end controlled on the dock side by the canal company's staff.

We picked up the pilot at 13:00 hours and then proceeded to pass down the canal to the first group of locks at Gatun. This was very exciting and an amazing experience! We were accompanied in the locks by a large bulk cargo ship, taking up the full width of the lock. We were the only yacht in the lock. All proceeded well, controlled by constant communication via our pilot with the lock controllers. Marilyn, at home in Kefalonia was able to watch us live on the webcam which is sited over the lock.

Shortly before sunset we exited the first part of the canal and took up a buoy in the beautiful calm Gatun lake. Here the pilot left us and then our little party of five sat out on the deck and enjoyed each other's company and the twilight evening sharing bottles of wine, beer and even a little rum together. I prepared a prawn salad followed by the meal which had been pre-prepared by the Shelter Bay restaurant. After our supper the party carried on late into the night. It was a beautiful end to an exciting day, for me very stressful but also so much fun. I was so grateful to be with such a great group of people, out on the lake with Beebee and Grace. The Caribbean and the Atlantic oceans were now well behind us.

The following morning I cooked bacon and eggs for our breakfast and once the new pilot arrived, we set off to re-enter the canal and proceed once again towards the Pacific Ocean at the Balboa end. Mike made us delicious sandwiches for lunch whilst under way and we were a cheerful happy group of people. It seemed that everyone slept quite well in spite of the heat during the night. I was able to provide everyone with a clean towel, clean sheets and two pillows from my onboard stocks, much to my relief.

Following lunch we entered the last stretch of the canal and proceeded to the Guillard locks, the highest lift on the canal. We were once again the only yacht in the locks but we were accompanied by a very large Japanese car carrier which totally dwarfed us in height and took up the full width of the lock, with only a few feet on either side to spare, between the side of the ship and the very rough concrete of the lock sides! This vessel was as high out of water as a modern cruise ship and I did wonder if the crew were aware of our presence way down below its deck. I remember Malcolm Williams saying *"Here we have Grace and there we have the Graceless"*. This was, I thought, a very fitting description of this monumental metal floating box.

"Here we have Grace and there we have the Graceless"
the monumental metal floating box in one of the
Panama locks

In due course we passed under the "Bridge of the Americas", a high level road and rail bridge spanning the canal, and arrived at the yacht club, where the taxi was waiting to take my newly made friends back to Shelter Bay. The pilot had left us just ten minutes before, having been collected by the service vessel and taken ashore.

We docked Grace at the club, had our last beer together bought by Mike and then said our farewells. I was very sad to lose my new found friends, and also because this was the first time that I had people on board helping to sail Grace and share the hard work, and so leaving the dock with only me and Beebee after such an emotional high, was very sad. It had been a lot of fun, stress and quite an amazing two days. I motored Grace out into the channel and anchored behind the causeway linking an island to the mainland. In the darkening twilight I all at once felt sad and lonely but pleased that the transit had been completed without any problems, but also amazed that we are now in the Pacific Ocean!

BEYOND THE SUNSET

10

Pacific Ocean to the Galapagos Islands

At 13:30 hours left the anchorage in hot sunny weather. I motored Grace down the buoyed channel in a windless afternoon having spent the morning getting the boat ocean ready.

By early evening a westerly wind had picked up and we were now sailing down the Gulf of Panama at six knots under full rig, the weather remaining very warm in spite of the wind.

There was a lot of shipping about all proceeding in the same direction as we were so I decided it would be prudent to sail outside the channel on a parallel heading, about one mile off. I was very sad because I had not been able to use the time left on my phone to call Marilyn, as we had arranged when I last spoke to her from Christobal. It seemed that there was a fault with the phone, possibly the battery connection.

BEYOND THE SUNSET

Sunday 11th September 2016 Day 2
09:00 hours N 07 27 W 79 34
wind S W very light overcast
sea slight swell
heading 225 magnetic

Becalmed, so I am running the engine making five knots. The night kept me busy as there was always at least four ships on the A.I.S. radar at any one time, most on a parallel course of 180 magnetic.

At noon the wind remained almost non-existent but we nevertheless have managed to do 80 miles since 13:30 hours yesterday, it seems that we had a good push from the current last night. By 16:00 hours the wind has picked up to a south west fresh breeze of fifteen knots and the sea is quite lumpy, leaving me no choice but to motor against it on a heading of 270 magnetic.

Monday 12th September 2016 Day 3
Baloa 151 miles
11:00 Hours N 06 24 W 80 13
wind light variable sea light
heading 200 magnetic at 2 knots

We are surrounded by rain on all around horizons, making a slow two knots to windward over a one metre swell. I debated whether to run the motor but decided that only if the boat speed drops below two knots, would I start the engine. At 17:00 hours we left the Gulf of Panama and changed our heading, now pointing Grace towards the Galapagos Islands, about 800 miles away.

Tuesday 13th September 2016 Day 4
08:00 hours N 05 17 W 80 25
wind light W sea 0-1 metre swell overcast
heading 200 magnetic

Today we are sailing at 2.5 knots with the engine off and the weather slightly improved on yesterday but still occasional rain. I searched through my charts to find one which will cover the next leg to the Marquesas Islands, but to no avail, so will have to Captain Cook it, that is, he made Pacific charts as he sailed across the Pacific, he was the first to do this.

We are settling down to a routine and accept that from here to the Galapagos the wind is notoriously light. I slept through the night yesterday without keeping any watch as the A.I.S. radar has shown no shipping for the last two days. I am enjoying the quiet life now, particularly in comparison with the previous two weeks. We have a long sail ahead of us to the Marquesas, around six weeks if I don't stop in the Galapagos, which I probably won't, as the cost of permits is quite high, unless shared amongst a group.

At 16:00 hours I logged that life is now easy after a hard five weeks since leaving the Virgin Islands. We are now 233 miles from Panama.

Wednesday 14th September 2016 Day 5
08:00 hours N 04 35 W 80 45
no wind flat sea overcast engine on
doing 5 knots at 1,000 rpm

Even though our progress is slow, I am not
concerned, because I am enjoying the peace and lack of
stress that was so much part of my stay in Panama and
before. Here we are slowly gliding across the big wide
ocean with very little to concern us. I made up my own
chart this morning so as to be able to plot my position as
we go and therefore see our relative position to the
Galapagos islands. Another chore that I was able to tackle
quite successfully today was the tightening of the Aries
brackets which had become loose.

Thursday 15th September 2016 Day 6
09:30 hours
Run 69 miles
wind SW 10-15 knots sea 1 metre swell
overcast heading 260 magnetic

We are making four knots on course for our weigh
point, carrying reefed main and reduced staysail and jib.
We had heavy rain all last evening and so I hove-to at
midnight as I know that we are in the vicinity of a small
island (Marpelo) which shows as a pin head sized dot on
the only chart I have, this stretches from the Americas to
Australia, so a very large scale. I have plotted it on my

homemade chart but can't be sure of its position within twenty miles, so decided to wait for daylight, just in case. I worked out months later after getting its position from the internet, that we had passed about thirty miles to the west of it.

At noon the recorded wind was south, south-west at fifteen knots, with a swell of one to two metres and some occasional rain. We have made sixty nine miles in twenty four hours which I am pleased with, as windward passage making is always difficult in any kind of seaway.

Friday 16th September 2016 Day 7
09:00 hours N 04 24 W 82 24
wind variable light rain and overcast

I noticed that we seemed to be fighting a current which is in the same direction as these headwinds. It is probable that to cross this current stream we would have to get down to two degrees north of the equator or even further south!

Saturday 17th September 2016 Day 8
N 03 31 W 82 52

We are still pushing against this current and there is still no wind. It was cold overnight and I think this current is the likely cause and possibly the cause of this windless continuous overcast, rainy weather. At noon I note in the log that we are making four knots with the engine on idle.

Sunday 18th September 2016 Day 9
07:00 hours N 02 24 W 82 13
wind W S-W 10-15 knots sea 1 metre
overcast and cool sailing
150 magnetic at 2 knots

At 10:00 hours the sun managed to make an appearance and we were sailing close hauled at just over two knots. The other tack would put us on a heading of 260 magnetic but I really wanted to be heading more south so as to get out of this cold current and into the south Equatorial current which flows along the equator.

One week at sea now with dismal progress to show for it. When we have had wind it has always been on the nose. It is time for a change, as I am actually heading on this tack away from the Galapagos but if I steer for these islands I go straight into the counter current. Hence, I need to cross the equator first.

For the next 6 days the weather mostly alternated from calm to wind on the nose and it was quite surprisingly cool as we approached the equator. The wind when we had it was very light but not unpleasant sailing as the sea was mostly pretty flat.

Our daily runs never exceeded 90 miles but averaged around 60 to 80 and which was not too bad as it was always to windward.

Our diesel situation is low and our food stocks can

always be topped up, so I have decided to make a stopover in Wreck Bay, in the Galapagos islands.

Having time for contemplation has made me cast my mind back to the time before I started this circumnavigation, particularly as I am now in the Pacific Ocean, having completed the Panama Canal transit. These have been my dreams for so long and now, I am living these dreams and approaching the Galapagos.

But what had finally made me cut loose from a settled, relaxed life on the beautiful Greek island of Kefalonia where I have my permanent home with Marilyn?

11

2014 The sinking of Grace

As I have previously said, the need to sail around the world has been a long-held ambition of mine but as we all know, in life our plans are often thwarted by changing circumstances. And before we know it, we find ourselves becoming trapped by our routines and life's comforts and all this time the clock runs without pause and just like Rip Van Winkle, we wake up and find that we are living in the last quarter of our life span. This is where I found myself by 2014 and so I decided I to think seriously of going sooner rather than later as I was in my late 60s. I ordered the charts and started to plan for a departure the following year. Grace was after all in good condition and had returned from a run to the Caribbean and back in 2012.

My house on Kefalonia which I built, was finally completed and Grace had a free birth in the local marina, as the municipality could not find investors to complete and run it as a business. This was an ideal situation for me and I was also now getting my old age pension.

In late June, I was on my way to clean a swimming pool which I looked after, when Marilyn phoned me in a highly emotional state to say, *"Get down to Spartia Bay as quick as you can as Grace is on the rocks*!" This message filled me with dread and panic, my brain seem to become paralysed. Now, I had laid a mooring for Grace in Spartia Bay, so I could readily board her most days from the beach, which is only 2 miles from my house. On arrival at the bay I found about 30 people standing on the rocks, mostly holiday makers with a few locals looking at the spectacle of a sunken yacht in 2 meters of water!

Grace sunken in Spartia Bay

She was lying at about thirty degrees and it was plainly obvious that she was mortally holed and stuck firmly on the rocks. This was my worst nightmare, a situation that I had no previous experience in dealing with, having never before being involved in a similar situation. I was paralysed with total panic – how was I to save Grace? The authorities had already been summoned by the locals, who feared for the contamination of the beach. The authorities immediately questioned me on the quantity of fuel and oil on board the boat and naturally I minimised this to a few litres and I must confess that this was the least of my concerns.

A salvage team had also arrived, called in by the port authorities for the island, and I found their presence most reassuring. I had in the meantime started to try and salvage my possessions which were floating around the boat. On boarding the boat I found the interior covered in black engine oil which had floated out from the engine and lay in a thick layer on the surface of the water, which filled the boat to thirty centimetres from the ceiling.

When I returned to the beach the salvage team said that they were unable to proceed with any salvage work that day, but would return the following day to assess the situation. They had discovered two large holes, measuring around sixty centimetres across caused by the rocks penetrating the hull. It was also their opinion that even the largest crane on the island would not be able to lift Grace because they could not stand the crane close enough to the boat, but would consult with a crane company about dragging the boat closer, before attempting a lift. This would or course, cause even more damage to the hull as she was lying amongst a group of boulders.

They felt that the boat could possibly be recovered intact and placed on a truck, but would there be enough left of her to justify the expense? Nevertheless, I as the owner of the sunken boat was responsible for clearing all the wreckage off this popular tourist beach.

For me this was soul destroying. Here lay Grace, the boat which had sailed across the Atlantic and through the Bahamas with Marilyn and I. It had been our home for three years. We had anchored in front of the Statue of Liberty in New York harbour and had been to Canada and then back to Florida again. Both my children, Fiona and Neil, had sailed extensively on Grace and I had done four solo Atlantic crossings in her. From those early days on the farm when Marilyn and I had rebuilt her until now, had eclipsed fifteen years of our lives. Surely this was not her unfitting, undignified end?

The following day the salvage team returned with the largest crane that could be found on the island. Graham, my good friend on the island, his son Bradley and other British ex-patriots all came down to help and we quickly released the mast and boom from the deck and these were craned on to the shore. A diver fixed the strops from the crane under the hull and then the crane managed to pull Grace back to the vertical, so that now she was once again upright on her iron keel on the rocks. From this position she was dragged over the rocks, about ten metres closer to the shore, sliding all the time on her iron keel. This was a tribute to Ted her original builder, because if the keel was not well secured to the hull it would break away.

The first lift attempt failed, so a second crane was brought from Argostoli to hold down the back of the primary crane, which was rising up when an attempt to lift

Grace was made. After this was set up the crane operators with great skill, slowly raised her out of the water and held her at the surface whilst tons of water poured from the huge holes in the hull. A little while later they were able to swing her onto the roadway and there we chocked her up to wait for the truck, which was to take the boat to the marina. Except for the large holes in the hull caused by the rocks, she was surprisingly undamaged, only a few minor scrapes which were very superficial. The interior was covered in thick engine oil on every surface, and needless to say, all electrical equipment was destroyed.

My emotional state had roller coastered from extreme anxiety to relief and I knew that nothing would stop me from repairing Grace and there was no doubt in my mind that we would sail again!

Once the truck arrived, Grace was secured on the back and we began our journey through the villages to the marina where I knew I could store the boat next to the water, repair her and then it would be an easy lift to put her back in the water before moving the boat back to her long time berth.

As the truck started this journey, with me riding on the back, a large group of English holiday makers, who had spent the morning watching the salvage operation, stood together and clapped in applause. They had seen the ragged Union Jack red ensign still intact, hanging on the stern of the boat.

Some months later, when I dived on the mooring to recover my equipment, I was horrified to discover that both the chain and rope had been cut at the water level. This was now the trigger which made me decide to circumnavigate Grace as soon as possible, to escape to the safety of an ocean voyage.

The following week work was started on the repairs and knowing that I had many months of labour ahead of me. Mike Knott an English carpenter, who lived on the island came down to the boat to help me for the first few weeks. He was a good friend of mine and he realised that his help and his presence was necessary to get me going again. But once we started, I could not find enough hours in the day. The work was very therapeutic, enjoyable and deeply satisfying. I thanked God for my skills and drive to recreate this brave little boat.

12

The Galapagos Islands

25th September 2016 Day 16
08:00 hours N 00 16 W 89 21
wind S SW 5-10 knots
sea half metre swell light rain
heading 230 magnetic making 2 knots

We are still 16 miles from the equator and 70 miles from Wreck Bay. The wind remained light but steady overnight, which kept us moving. Grace has managed 75 miles since yesterday, but the wind is still on the nose which is preventing me from steering directly for Wreck Bay and the situation is not improved by the strong westerly set in the current. By 12:00 hours the wind had become fresh and is now blowing up to 20 knots making our heading quite impossible.

I decide at this stage to do a food and water check on our stocks and came to the conclusion that we had enough to get us to the Marquesas, part of French Polynesia, our next destination. Based on this encouraging stock check I turned the boat on a direct heading to the Marquesas. We have no luxuries or fresh food remaining on board and our diesel stocks are very low, but the alternative would take days against this current and wind to make a land fall at Wreck Bay. I turned the boat to our new heading of 270 degrees magnetic, now with the wind and current in our favour we are roaring along at 7 knots, our fastest speed since Panama.

Nuku Hiva, our destination is 3,000 miles away, so Beebee and I will have to endure another month at sea before we see land again!

Monday 26th September 2016 Day 17
08:00 hours N 00 05 W 90 49
light rain poor visibility
becalmed heading 270 magnetic
current 1 knot westerly set

After a marvellous reach on the equator from noon yesterday, doing 8 knots at times we lost the wind at 18:00 hours, nevertheless we were able to maintain steerage in the light wind, sailing at 2 knots, plus a bonus from the current of 1 knot.

At noon, the rain cleared and we welcomed the sun and much improved visibility. The island of Isa Bella was starkly visible on our port side 15 miles away.

Nuku Hiva in French Polynesia is 2,968 miles away. I feel very disappointed on leaving the Galapagos without stopping, but I am happy that I have made the right decision.

Tuesday 27th September 2016 Day 18
N 00 07 W 92 13
Run 90 miles
wind S W 10-15 knots sea slight overcast
light rain cold heading 270 magnetic

After being becalmed yesterday the wind picked up at 20:00 hours and I spent the evening until 01:00 hours trying to avoid the unlit island which is west of Isabella. Because I don't have a chart covering this area it was necessary to keep a careful vigil until I was quite sure this island was well behind us.

At 08:30 hours the Galapagos Islands are now 70 miles behind us and we are 2,916 miles from Nuku Hiva, making a steady 4.5 knots on a good heading. Last night was cold requiring extra bedding on my bunk. At noon I claim a run of 90 miles which really was not bad as most had been to windward.

We are now well on our way to the Marquesas and I write in the log that the Chilean authorities should be held to account for keeping these islands unlit. They do not seem to have any lighthouses and on some of the islands there are no lights on shore from habitation. This poses a hazard to shipping and yachtsmen.

I am worried about a vibration on the propeller shaft that could have been caused by the boat running into surface long lines three days ago. These long lines are laid out with baited hooks to catch tuna and can be five miles or more long, and in my opinion they are another way of destroying the world's fish stocks not to mention the discarding of these lines becoming a huge pollutant to the oceans.

I am now hoping for better weather as the trip from Panama was basically rainy and with windward sailing most of the way, I feel that I am owed a change at this time. It could have been a lot easier and more pleasant with a few more sunny days.

Wednesday 28th September 2016 Day 19

Run 89 miles

S 00 14 W 93 35

Nuku Hiva 2830 miles

wind S E 10 knots sea slight overcast cool

heading 240 magnetic at 4 knots

We enjoyed a beautiful, gentle sail from 15:00 hours and all through the night, although it did cool down in the evening and overnight. This south east wind could be the start of the trade winds!

We have achieved 89 miles since noon yesterday and have crossed the equator into the South Pacific Ocean. My intention is to sail down to the vicinity of 10 degrees south, where we should get better and stronger south east winds. At noon I write in the logbook that the south east wind is giving us a good beam reach and we are doing as much as seven knots, though there is a possibility that one of those might just be from the current.

Thursday 29th September 2016 Day 20
Run 79 miles
S 00 45 W 95 11
Nuku Hiva 2,741 miles
wind S E 10 knots sea flat overcast
heading 220 magnetic

We lost the wind completely from midnight until 08:00 hours today, so we had no option but to drift. This morning I have started work on the old spare genoa from the previous mast, to try and make it fit the new mast because the one which I had bought in Spain to fit the new mast, is starting to fall apart in any sort of wind. Today I caught a 3 kilos yellow fin tuna, which I filleted, eating one fillet for dinner and the other will be tomorrows breakfast. Sadly, I had to throw away the rest, as without refrigeration on board it would not keep.

30th September 2016 Day 21
Run 79 miles
S 00 45 W 96 22
Wind S E 8-10 knots sea flat overcast
Nuku Hiva 2,662 miles

Grace kept sailing all night at steerage speed but at the very least we were moving and Aries steered without fault. The morning is overcast but hopefully it will clear later. There is a possibility that, as we are now 45 miles south of the equator that the south east wind might strengthen. I have turned Grace more into the wind to try and get better speed from its low strength so we are now sailing at 220 magnetic. It seems that we have now lost the equatorial current, so hopefully the winds will continue to improve until 5 degrees south, which is 300 miles south of the equator.

Today is my 69th birthday, one of many that I have spent at sea. I share this birthday with an old friend of mine, Syd Templeton, who tragically was killed 27 years ago, a great fellow Rhodesian.

1st October 2016 Day 22

Run 68 miles

S 01 05 W 97 25

Nuku Hiva 2594 miles

wind S E 8-10 knots overcast sea slight

speed 3 knots at 240 magnetic

Light winds yesterday and overnight have given us a low run of only 68 miles. We are now sixty-five miles south of the equator but it seems there is little or no Equatorial current where we are.

Yesterday I took down the genoa which is constantly tearing even in the slightest wind, so now I am waiting for a really calm day so that I can replace it with my old genoa from the previous mast. I have enlarged the bolt tape to fit my new roller furling foil by gluing on a double thickness of sunbrella, which I think will work.

Marilyn sent me a text message on my satellite tracker yesterday wishing me a happy birthday. This little message gave me a good feeling which lasted for hours.

2nd October 2016 Day 23
Run 80 miles
09:00 hours S 01 18 W 98 45
Nuku Hiva 2,514 miles wind S E 15-20 knots
sea 1-2 metre sunny
heading 260 magnetic making 6 knots

A very pleasant sunny morning with a fresh south east wind driving Grace at 6 knots over a building sea. The weather had become squally overnight keeping me busy at times, but I am not complaining as our run has improved after our slow passage in yesterday's light winds. This is the strongest wind we are having since Panama!

I worked all yesterday afternoon putting up the old genoa, taking the opportunity in the very light wind and now it is on and I managed to keep it working all night. It is a huge improvement on the old Spanish genoa which was a strange shape and was never very suitable for Grace.

At noon I recorded our run of 80 miles and at 17:00 hours I stated in the log that the wind was now 20 knots southerly and we were making a generous six knots giving us good mileage for the day.

Monday 3rd October 2016 Day 24
Run 97 miles
07:30 hours S 01 27 W 100 24
wind S squally sea 1-2 metres
overcast cold heading 260 magnetic at 5 knots

The squally conditions kept me busy through the night but even so, I am hoping for our first 100 mile run since Panama. We are now one week from the Galapagos Islands having sailed 553 miles in this period.

Yesterday was a lazy day reading and also watching the television series "House" on my computer. I was very cross with myself when I lost a winch handle overboard whilst reefing the mainsail during the night. What makes this so annoying is that this is the second one that I have lost in two days, so I have decided to look carefully at my routine to ensure that this does not happen again. I still have two spares but the best ones that I had are now on the Pacific seabed.

Tuesday 4th October 2016 Day 25
Run 110 miles
07:30 hours S 01 58 W 102 05
Nuku Hiva 2,310 miles
wind S SE 15 knots overcast sea 1 metre
occasional rain heading 250 magnetic at 6 knots

Our noon run of 110 miles has been a record since Panama, which is very pleasing but to push up our average, we would need runs like this more frequently, to make up for the past light winds. We are definitely now in the trade winds which the south Pacific is famous for amongst yachtsmen, so being nearly 120 miles south of the equator is definitely paying off.

Wednesday 5th October 2016 Day 26
Run 100 miles
08: 00 hours S 02 30 W 103 43
Nuku Hiva 2,206 miles wind S SE 10-15 knots
sunny sea 1 metre
heading 250 magnetic at 5-6 knots

We were becalmed for 3 hours overnight and experienced light winds to midnight all of which has reduced our run to 100 miles, which I am pleased with when all is considered. From 03:00 the wind picked up and kept fresh until 08:00 but I must confess I was in a deep sleep, so we were probably doing a good speed, thus explaining our better than expected run.

At 11:00 hours I record in the log that were enjoying a lovely sail at 6 knots over a calm sea in a 10 knots breeze, so I have concluded that we must be benefiting from the south equatorial current and this would explain the better than expected run overnight.

We are nearly half-way from Panama to the Marquesas but still over three weeks to go. This part of the sail has now become very enjoyable, all that was expected from the South Pacific.

Our food stocks seem to be adequate to get us to our destination but nevertheless I must remain frugal with both mine and Beebee's food. My concern is with the staples like pasta, rice and crackers. The rum will run out in four days, I do enjoy a tot of rum with a splash of lime juice and a teaspoon of brown sugar on a daily basis. Our sugar will also run out in about four days. One jar of jam remains but we no longer have any luxuries like nuts, sweet biscuits or dried fruit. Cooking gas should last another thirty days at least and we have two months of water on board.

The sailing now is very easy and relaxing and as I have always said, I would rather sail at 5 knots under full sail than 7 knots carrying double reefs.

13

A long sail to French Polynesia

Monday 10th October 2016 Day 31
Run 96 miles
09:00 hours S 05 32 W 110 58
wind SE 15 knots sunny sea 1 metre
heading 230 magnetic some rain squalls

During the last 24 hours we made more southing from our rhumb line course because we had been sailing on a beam reach. This reduced our gain to Nuku Hiva, giving us a 24 hour run of 96 miles, even though we actually sailed 105 miles. I am really grateful for these stronger winds, which is what I had hoped for at this latitude.

At noon I write in the log that I spent the morning doing a food inventory and I am relieved to find that our stocks are not as bad as I previously thought and furthermore it seems we have food for another 20 days. Hopefully we should be in the Marquesas in 16 days as we have 1,700 miles remaining.

I have decided to ensure that Beebee sleeps below decks at night as previously I allowed her to remain in the cockpit, which was always her preference. One of my greatest fears, would be to come up on deck in the morning and find no Beebee. This would devastate me and make the continuation of this circumnavigation almost unbearable. Beebee and I have always been close, as she is such a well-behaved intelligent dog, who has no faults. She is totally obedient and fully understands her place in my life and on the boat. We have deep understanding and people who see us together always comment that they are sure we speak the same language. To this I agree, as Beebee and I spend all our lives together and have done so ever since she first came into my life when she was just a year old.

Sunday 16th October 2016 Day 37
Run 89 miles
South 07 16 W 120 21
wind v light 0-5 E sunny hot
motoring at 240 magnetic

This is the first time since the Galapagos that we are having to run the engine as we have no wind. Our sailing for the last week has been slow but very relaxing on calm seas, even though the wind has been light, we have maintained steerage. Beebee has got used to spending the nights below deck now which gives much peace of mind. We are currently enjoying a wonderful full moon giving a beautiful sepia cast to the gentle swell of the ever-moving vast sea.

Sailing across the Pacific to the Marquesas has been my dream for many years and now here I am doing just that, giving me a feeling of quiet contentment. This is my third serious attempt to do this and I feel quite privileged to have this ability and opportunity to sail the Pacific, particularly at my age which often brings on nervousness and negativity preventing one from enjoying to the full, the latter years of life.

I am now plotting my position on a proper printed chart titled "South East Polynesia," instead of on the chart which I had made myself so it is very satisfying to see our position and our destination on the same chart. We will soon be less than a thousand miles from Nuka Hiva.

Wednesday 19th October 2016 Day 40
run 102 miles
09:00 hours S 08 10 W 124 20
Nuka Hiva 937 miles
wind 15-30 knots squally sea rough
heading 240 magnetic double reefed

At noon I recorded in the log that we are running on a port tack with the pole boomed out carrying a tiny genoa and in spite of our double reef we are surfing down the waves at full hull speed.

Wind at last, so I cannot be too choosy but it is gratifying to have once again done a 100 mile run. This squally wind is keeping me busy and it is now three weeks since we passed the Galapagos Islands. I noted in the log that I have had to work hard for this 100 miles run from the early hours when the wind suddenly picked up but at last we are less than one thousand miles to Nuka Hiva.

Thursday 20th October 2016 Day 41

Run 100 miles

07:30 hours S 08 17 W 125 59

Nuka Hiva 839 miles

wind 15/20E sea rough overcast

heading 220 magnetic

We are still double reefed from yesterday's strong winds which were gusting at gale force during the night but today have calmed down and I am expecting our light trade winds to return. I anticipate shaking out the reefs before night fall.

I look forward to setting Grace on a broad reach again because this rolling which always accompanies a dead run is uncomfortable and tiring.

At 17:00 hours I am able to improve our heading in a very steady 15 knot wind, once again on full main and genoa. Nuku Hiva is now 839 miles away and on examination of our food stocks I see now that there is no reason to worry about our food stocks running out. We are 41 days at sea without stopping, this is now approaching our record of 42 days.

Saturday 22nd October 2016 Day 43
Run 110 miles
08:00 hours S 08 24 W 129 27
wind E-NE 10-20 knots sea moderate sunny
running at 270 magnetic poled out on port tack

I had trouble getting Aries to work well during the night so getting a good night's sleep was not on the cards. As the wind is blowing south of east, we have gained in our northing by 14 miles in 24 hours which is pleasing as this puts us on the latitude of Nuku Hiva. By noon the wind has become a little fresher and I record our run at 110 miles in 24 hours which is our first 100 plus run since the 4th October. At 17:00 hours I have noted that we have maintained a steady 5-6 knots all afternoon making today another perfect sailing day

Sunday 23rd October 2016 Day 44
Run 117 miles
12:00 hours S 08 54 W 131 48
Nuku Hiva 492 miles
wind NE 15 knots sunny sea moderate heading 240
magnetic on run

The wind swing overnight has put us a further 10 miles south but a steady 15 knot wind kept Aries working without requiring any attention and giving us another good run of 118 miles on course even though we actually sailed 121 miles. This is another record for this leg which is very pleasing.

It took me an hour to put Grace over on to the starboard tack, our first time with the wind on the starboard side since the Galapagos islands on a full rig. It seems all good things must come to an end, so by 17:00 hours the wind has dropped and now we are sailing just above steerage speed.

I feel now that I am much more competent at sailing Grace with her new mast. She is a different boat and to sail her in lighter winds with her reduced sail plan requires new understandings. It is also the working relationship between the sail plan and Aries which is what it is all about, keeping as much sail up as possible without putting the boat out of balance. Aries is a powerful auto-pilot, but was designed nearly 60 years ago, Modern electric and hydraulic powered auto-pilots are more powerful and can oversteer bad weather with more sail up, thus making more speed, but the downside is that they do require a lot of electric power, whereas Aries uses no electric power whatsoever, using only energy provided by the wind.

We are now only 513 miles from our destination, so we count the days remaining on one hand and no longer think in weeks.

Monday 24th October 2016 Day 45
run 98 miles
08:00 hours S 08 38 W 133 09
Nuka Hiva 413 miles
wind E-NE 15 knots cloudy sea moderate
heading 270 magnetic on run
pole on starboard side full main and genoa

Our noon run of 98 miles is not too bad as the wind yesterday afternoon and evening was light. Today the wind is fresh NE and is great for making mileage, we are averaging 5 knots. I have just realised that we have done over 600 miles in the last 6 days, which is very satisfying. Of course, I know that modern boats would do a thousand miles in 6 days in these conditions. On recount I make it 700 miles in 7 days, even better!

The days now are much hotter, as are the nights and Beebee is feeling the heat, but now we have only days to go to Nuku Hiva, so everything is bearable. We are in the 300s and I feel very content and I know I must enjoy this countdown to our arrival, as I will never experience this land fall again, our very first in the Pacific Ocean. Obviously, this can only be beaten by a land fall in Kefalonia on Grace, but at this time that seems a long way off. Many miles lie ahead and knowing all the problems and hazards that sailing an old wooden boat single handed entails, I dare not dream of the future.

Tuesday 25th October 2016 Day 46

Run 90 miles

08:00 hours S 08 16 W 134 48

Nuku Hiva 262 miles

wind NE 15 knots sea moderate

sunny

good heading 300 magnetic at 5 knots

broad reach since 18:00 hours last night

Last night it was quite rough so I hoped for a better run. We did make 22 miles north in the last 24 hours which is good, as I do not want to have to make a windward approach to Nuka Hiva.

Our noon recorded run was only 90 miles in spite of the fresh wind, which I found disappointing. At 15:00 hours the wind dropped a little so I am really hoping that it picks up overnight instead of the normal trend of becoming lighter at night.

Forty six days at sea now, so it will be a 50 day trip-food is just about lasting. The water tank is now empty but I still have 50 litres in containers. Beebee's food is good for 3 weeks but alcohol (rum) ran out 2 weeks ago, which surprisingly I do not miss as much as I thought I would, nevertheless a lovely cold beer would be truly wonderful.

It looks like a Friday land fall might be possible if the weather is kind to us. We should be less than 300 miles this evening but on reconsideration I must make every effort to land fall on Friday, as so often the authorities are closed on weekends preventing me going ashore until Monday.

At 17:00 hours I write in the log that Grace is moving along gently at 4-5 knots over a sunny blue sea. A fishing trawler is visible on the horizon and this is the first vessel of any description that I have seen in a month.

Wednesday 26th October 2016 Day 47

Run 96 miles

08:00 hours S 07 54 W 136 21

Wind E 10-15 sea slight sunny

heading 270 magnetic

I was a little disappointed in out overnight run but as always the winds became light overnight.
With the coming of sunrise the wind has strengthened to 10 to 15 knots, becoming easterly and we are now on a downwind run on a starboard tack with full genoa on the spinnaker pole.

Aries has performed surprisingly well over the past week, ever since I changed the plywood vane to a larger one. We are 20 miles north of our track, so I must stop this trend, as it seems the wind is staying North of East so maybe I should position Grace to be slightly South of Nuka Hiva.

I had my last cup of sweet coffee as the sugar stocks are now finished. We do not have jam, honey or anything sweet except for baked beans. So now, we are really out of real luxuries. Our remaining stocks are rice, tinned vegetables, baked beans, cheap tinned fish, dried beans, pasta and tomato puree. Oh not to forget two tins of Vienna sausages, four packets of noodles, which is junk food but tasty. Coffee, tea and milk are still plentiful. There are enough crackers for breakfast today, but these are the last and no longer that fresh. Tomorrow and Friday's breakfast will either be noodles or rice.

We are almost a month from the Galapagos islands, which was our last sight of land. Time has passed so quickly. I think if the weather had been bad the trip would have seemed so much longer but because of these pleasant sailing days, watching videos and reading for hours each day, time has flown by and no sooner had I turned to a new page in the logbook, it seems that I am already turning the page again to the next day.

At noon I read on the GPS that the run in 96 miles for the 24 hours from noon yesterday.

Thursday 27th October 2016 Day 48
Run 98 miles
08:00 hours S 08 18 W 137 49
Nuku Hiva 141 wind E 8-12 sea slight sunny
heading 240 magnetic at 4 knots

The wind over night and yesterday afternoon was very light and our boat speed barely adequate to maintain steerage, so I was quite surprised to see that we had done 90 miles since 08:00 hours yesterday. This leaves 140 miles to Nuku Hiva, which is possible before dark tomorrow in these light wind conditions. Dare I say it, but the wind this morning has pushed the boat speed up to 4.5 knots from the 2-3 knots overnight. We are still carrying the full genoa on our port side.

Our noon run gives up 98 miles but sadly during the afternoon the wind is dropping and by 18:00 hours we are becalmed. This is all I need with our land fall only 24 hours away after 49 days at sea. During the day I once again felt very dizzy and started to lose my balance and found myself staggering as if I had drunk a pint of rum. This is the second time it has happened in the last two weeks.

I started the engine, using our precious diesel, which I am so disinclined to do, as the engine is a necessary requirement to make our land falls when approaching land, rocks and reefs. Vibration became immediately apparent, so after examination I found a loose engine mount. This I was quickly able to tighten up and I was very pleased with myself for my rapid analysis.

I dragged some laundry in the sea again as I will need some clothes to wear ashore, the saltiness in the clothes after drying does not bother me, but a rain squall to give a fresh rinse is always welcome.

Friday 28th October 2016 Day 49
Run 90 miles
07:00 hours S 08 36 W 139 16
Nuku Hiva 57 miles
wind light 0-10 E sea calm sunny
motor sailing at 245 magnetic

In spite of running the engine on our precious diesel fuel for 12 hours yesterday, we still only managed a run of 90 miles from 08:00 hours to 08:00 hours today, due to very light winds of only 5-10 knots, giving us a speed of 2 knots. So, to make Nuku Hiva in daylight today, I am now running the engine at 1,300 rpm giving us a speed of 6 knots.

Today is a very exciting day full of expectations, all around us the sky is dotted with a variety of bird life and Uahuka, one of the other islands in the group, is visible on the port bow, standing clear in the early morning light.

At noon we had only 20 miles to go but alas, still no wind and I anticipate I must soon shut down the engine to preserve our last few litres of diesel for our arrival. Nuku Hiva a high volcanic island is clearly visible ahead reaching high into the clouds. It is darkly green, dramatic and rugged in its beauty, a spectacular site after all these days at sea!

At 16:00 hours I shut down the engine and we slowly moved ahead at a snail's pace, barely making half a knot. I had to hand steer most of the time as Aries could not manage in the almost non-existent wind conditions. I do not think I have ever been more frustrated in my life!

I finally dropped anchor in Taiohae Bay on Saturday morning after taking 12 hours to sail the last 5 miles, having crept at glacial speed all night. I was too tired to feel jubilant but no sooner was the anchor down, my head hit the pillow, my last thoughts were at least it was not blowing a gale and I was fortunate that there was no rain whilst I sat in the open cockpit steering the boat

I awoke around 10 am, made myself a cup of coffee, took in the beautiful surroundings whilst Grace is lying quietly at anchor after 58 days of non-stop sailing. The island is high, rugged, very green and the buildings that I can see are low lying with no high-rise hotels and not clustered together but quite spread out amongst the tall tropical trees. The houses are modest single storey dwellings, clean and well maintained and the scenic beauty of it all, lying under the mountains is quite breath taking.

This is the most popular anchorage for yachtsman in the Marquesas, sailing from across the Pacific but alas I am not able to enjoy the social grouping of arriving yachts as I am too late in the season. The hurricane season is about to begin and I can only see 4 other yachts in the anchorage.

I launched the dinghy and rowed ashore carrying all my documents and Beebee's passport and vaccination certificates. I proceeded to go directly to the police station having been shown where it was by the very friendly locals.

The Police station is a small single storey brick

building, set on its own surrounded by well-manicured lawns and boarded by large beautiful Flamboyant trees with their widespread lush shady branches, sprinkled with amazing reddish orange flowers.

The clearing in process is uncomplicated except that I am required to copy all the forms to Tahiti. The police station is staffed by French police who are not Polynesian and are friendly and polite but nevertheless they would not send the documentation on my behalf to Tahiti. This proved difficult for me as I did not have a scanner or internet on board. So, I won't bother, nor explain this to the friendly man at the counter. Furthermore, I am horrified to be told that Beebee will not be allowed ashore, as there are no veterinary staff on the island to verify Beebee's health clearance and documentation.

This upset me enormously as one of the reasons Beebee travels with me is so that we can explore together and mutually enjoy long walks. She would normally accompany me everywhere and this includes the restaurants, supermarkets and bars. Beebee is totally well behaved, well trained and always happy to sit patiently outside a shop whilst I am buying our necessities. Now she has not been ashore for over 50 days and would dearly love to get her off of the boat for a good run. I am shocked as I had researched veterinary procedures for these islands and had understood that there would be facilities to check animals and their paperwork as long as they were chipped, vaccinated and carried all the correct documents. So, in theory, Beebee would have to stay on board all the time in the Marquesas.

I did our shopping in the village and enjoyed a cold beer at a bar where another couple, from a French yacht, were sitting.

After exploring the immediate area and doing some hikes I saw how clean, neat and well-groomed the town was, with pretty little houses set amongst there beautiful island foliage. The flora was colourful with bougainvillea and hibiscus in abundance, as well as tropical trees such as Flamboyant and Jacaranda making the whole area picture book perfect.

A couple of days later I moved Grace to the lovely Daniels Bay at the end of the island where I anchored under the towering cliffs in a beautiful very quiet serene location, this I shared with a French yacht. During the next few days I explored with Grace the other bays which were in easy access to the town, returning most nights.

On Saturday after stocking up with diesel, food and water I left Nuku Hiva from Daniels Bay at 16:00 hours heading for Tahiti. I am very sad to leave Nuku Hiva so soon as it is very beautiful, but expensive and also the cyclone season is now upon us. I need to get back to within 5 degrees of the equator to be out of the cyclone belt.

At 19:00 hours Nuku Hiva is now 10 miles behind us and fading into the twilight. I felt so sad because I had spent the last 35 years dreaming of visiting the Marquesas and now I am already passing through after such a short stay and frustrated at not being able to enjoy the islands with Beebee. So I feel I need to find another destination where I can take Beebee ashore.

14

French Polynesia

Sunday 6th November 2016
06:30 hours S 09 31 W 140 43
wind light NE sea slight
heading 250 magnetic
broad reach starboard tack

Nuku Hiva is now 52 miles behind us and Ua Pou is 37 miles on our quarter, barely visible in the clouds.

As always, I am hoping for more wind, which has been very light from midnight, making it difficult for Aries to maintain steerage. Around midnight the wind swung into the north, this requiring me to go on deck and gibe the boat on to the other tack. I set the sails for the best available performance instead of the direct heading to Tahiti.

At noon the wind became calm and this left me no choice but to start the engine, spoiling the tranquillity of our sail. The weather has remained mixed with sun and very light rain squalls.

BEYOND THE SUNSET

Monday 7th November 2016
07:00 hours S 09 39 W 141 44
wind calm variable sea slight
light rain and overcast

After motoring until 20:00 hours, I shut down the engine and we drifted in the calm until 07:00 hours this morning and once again I restarted the engine, continuing to motor at idle speed, making a steady 4 knots.

My intention is to head to a weigh point north of the Tuamoto Islands, then head for Tahiti in the Society Islands, thereafter to American Samoa. This is now the cyclone season, so the further south we are, the greater the danger from these violent storms and so it is my intention to work my way to Samoa, stopping wherever possible on the way to get weather up-dates. Luck does play a part in this plan as there are no real "hurricane holes" in the Tuamoto Islands or for that matter, in the Society Islands. A hurricane hole is a bay that offers good shelter in a cyclone from fierce winds and waves.

Basically, I am sailing too late in the season and I should have cut my stay in the Caribbean by a month, but I did want to spend as much time as possible with my family. Samoa does offer shelter from cyclones in the main town, Pago Pago as the bay is surrounded by hills on three sides and the entrance is a windy route protected behind an extensive reef.

FRENCH POLYNESIA

Tuesday 8th November 2016
S 10 16 W 142 35
Tuamotus 474 miles
wind W-SW 5-10 knots sea slight
overcast and rain squalls motor-sailing
240 magnetic at 4 knots

As usual we were becalmed overnight and drifted from 20:00 hours until 05:00 hours today at which time I started the engine. Our drift was towards the west which must be from the current.

The wind remained very light and it drizzled all day, so we continued to motor sail, although I do not think we got much push from the sails but nevertheless I kept them up.

Wednesday 9th November 2016
Run 90 miles
08:00 hours S 10 56 W 143 33
Tuamotu 404 miles
wind NW 10-15 knots rain drizzle
heading 230 magnetic at 4 knots

At 02:00 hours the wind returned and quickly became fresh north west giving us a better than expected noon run of 90 miles. This wind continued to strengthen in the afternoon and soon became 20-30 knots from the north west, driving Grace along at a very busy 6 knots, the fastest we have done in a long while. At 17:00 hours I write in the log that the sea has become rough and bouncy and Grace is surging forward at seven knots with the strong wind on the starboard beam, which is a fast point of sail for the boat. This very unsettled weather I believe is from a frontal system which has deprived us of the trade winds but there could also be a possibility that we are still in the doldrums.

Thursday 10th November 2016

Run 90 miles

S 12 14 W 144 39

wind 15-20 N sea rough overcast

heading 230 magnetic at 5-6 knots

single reef small genoa

I am quite disappointed in our run at noon of only 90 miles, as we sailed all night at five to six knots and today the wind remains fresh. Unfortunately, we also made too many miles to the south of our intended track, which puts our position closer to the Tuamotu Islands, a very extensive group of low lying islands barely one metre above sea level. These islands are surrounded by reefs and are poorly lit, so pose a great threat to lightly crewed and unwary passing yachts. They were known as the Dangerous Archipelago before the widespread use of GPS because they were so difficult to see and many unwary yachts paid dearly on the surrounding reefs. Even so, these islands do host many visiting boats every year because of the good diving on the reefs but the currents are strong within the lagoons and navigation in and out, always requires a man in the bows to keep a look out for coral heads. I want to pass to the north of the group by at least 35 miles to make sure that I am not on a lee shore should the weather become very bad.

At 17:00 hours the wind has dropped to 10–15 knots having remained squally with light rain all day accompanied by big swings in the wind direction. The sea situation has improved and now we are sailing at 3 knots on a broach reach. The horizon to the east is quite clear with a blue sky, so it looks like the weather system has blown through.

Friday 11th November 2016
Run 80 miles
wind calm sea slight sunny hot
heading 240 magnetic motoring

I am quite pleased with our noon position, giving us an 80 miles run, in spite of losing the wind at midnight, after a pleasant evening sail. The wind after midnight became very light, barely strong enough to keep Aries steering the boat.

This hot weather is great for drying out the boat and makes a very pleasant change from the damp drizzle that we have had to put up with. I am curious to know what will follow for the next week and naturally a steady trade wind all the way to Tahiti, would be a welcome change.

On this run I have not brought any alcohol on
board so Grace is a "dry boat". I am quite used to this now
and definitely feel happier and more cheerful without
alcohol, as booze does seem to have a depressing effect on
me. Furthermore, depression seems to take from life its
pleasures and joys in the beauty of things around us.

At 21:00 hours I turned off the engine, leaving the
boat to once again drift.

Saturday 12th November 2016

Run 60 miles

06:30 hours S 13 03 W 146 39

Tuamotus 178 miles

wind S 0-8 knots sunny sea flat motoring

After motoring very slowly to conserve fuel all
yesterday, making a modest 3–4 knots, we ended up
drifting through the night with the engine off. This allowed
me to catch up on sleep as Grace sat on a very flat sea in
bright moonlight, with no swell whatsoever. Under the
nearly full moon the stillness and tranquillity made it quite
magical.

Today we are now one week from Nuku Hiva, but
still 360 miles to Tahiti. I am presently re-reading all of
Patrick O'Brian's books, who was the greatest novelist of
18th century naval warfare. His books are based on actual
historical sea battles and his knowledge and accuracy of
those sailors and their ships is second to none. Having the
time to totally immerse myself in this literature is such a

luxury and gives me huge enjoyment. This is one of the wonderful things about ocean passage making that I love.

Sunday 13th November 2016
Run 60 miles
09:00 hours S 13 36 W 147 33
Tuamotus 118 miles
calm hot and sunny
heading 240 magnetic on engine

The sea is almost flat and once again we drifted most of the night with no wind but did manage one and a half hours sailing on a very light breeze, giving us steerage only. This trip is becoming very slow, here we are in the south east trade wind belt, yet day after day we experience little or no wind and I fear that this might continue through the summer.

Today I poured my last 25 litres drum of diesel into the fuel tank which will give me about 12 hours of motoring at idle speed.

Monday 14th November 2016
Tuamotus 79 miles
S 13 46 W 148 21
calm sunny sea flat drifting

We drifted the previous night with no wind at all, this being our fourth day without wind. To add insult to injury, we also drifted 13 miles north. I motored Grace most of yesterday at 700 rpm giving us a speed of 3 knots at a very low rate of fuel consumption. I have kept aside 20 litres for making our way into port. We could have carried more diesel but chose not to, as the price of diesel in the Marquesas was expensive, so I decided to preserve funds and wait on nature to provide the winds, which at times can be a long wait!

At noon I detect that we seem to have picked up a westerly set in the current of about 1.5 knots. I also record we are now 46 miles from our weigh point which means that we are now also 180 miles due north of Tahiti and on changing to a large scale chart, I see that Mataiva, our nearest Tuamotu Island is on our port beam about 25 miles away. I did not make any effort to try and see it because of its low height, it would be quite impossible to see it from the deck of Grace.

Tuesday 15th November 2016

08:00 hours S 14 28 W 149 00

wind w 5-10 knots sunny

very light swell

making 1-2 knots at 210 magnetic

This morning we are 22 miles from our Tuamotu weigh point and on our arrival there Grace will be re-set on a heading to Tahiti.

We motored until 15:00 hours and then I shut down the engine and we drifted until 17:00 hours whereupon a slight westerly breeze allowed us to commence sailing again.

Wednesday 16th November 2016

08:00 hours S 15 00 W 149 13

Tahiti 152 miles

wind 0–5 knots E large swell from SE

sunny drifting at 1 knot west direction

After a confused rainy night making only 10 miles, the wind today has come up from the south east, blowing very light at about five knots. The westerlies with their accompanying squalls have at last died away. These tiresome squally conditions have been obstinately persistent almost all the way from Nuku Hiva and the south east trades have been absent. We have made only 38 miles in 24 hours which is one of our slowest on record. I had hoped to be in Tahiti tomorrow but if these conditions persist, who knows when we will arrive?

The wind steadily picked up during the day and by early evening it was blowing at 15-20 knots driving Grace through a building sea at five plus knots. The eastern horizon now shows a very ominous belt of heavy dark blue, almost black clouds. This is a sure sign of an approaching strong squall or the onset of a storm, so it seems this swell from the south east which was present from the morning, was a definite sign of what was to come!

It did not take long before the wind became a shrieking banshee covering the boat in flying spray blown from huge two metre seas, which were quick to appear. I had taken warning from all the visual signs of an approaching storm and managed to get Grace treble reefed only minutes before being struck by the first blast of this gale force wind!

It did not take me long to set the boat to heave-to, putting her in a danger free mode so that she can ride out the gale in relative safety, a situation she has been in many times before.

07:00 hours 17th November 2016
Tahiti 133 miles
wind NE 15 knots sea rough overcast
heading 200 magnetic double reefed

From midnight the wind and waves began to drop and so I allowed myself the luxury of a few hours' sleep, knowing now that the worst was over. I awoke at dawn and seeing that the weather was decidedly improved, went on deck and set Grace sailing again under two reefs in the 25 knot wind on a course of 200 magnetic. By 11:00 hours the wind had returned to the south east and got stronger bringing big seas on to the beam. Big squalls were now blowing down on us at a frequent rate giving the seas little chance of calming down, making it difficult to make any headway. At 14:00 hours the huge beam seas left me no choice but to alter course away from Tahiti, heading now for Hua Hine, bringing the seas and the wind on to the quarter. Immediately our passage became much easier and we quickly picked up speed exceeding six knots at times, even though we were still double reefed!

The sea remained very rough all night, making sleep quite impossible, with Grace being thrown about until the first grey light of a troubled dawn. Determination made me keep on sailing and by mid-morning Hua Hine became visible through the grey squally clouds. At noon the sun finally made an appearance and the beautiful island appeared in the rapidly clearing sky. I dropped anchor in Fare anchorage at 13:00 hours after a very hard sail.

As we were still in French Polynesia, there were no arrival formalities to take care of and so spent the following day shopping in the small supermarket, as well as getting to know the other sailors anchored in the bay. There was an English family comprising of mum, dad and their 10 year old twin boys. Also, a charming young Australian couple, who were anchored closer to the reef to take advantage of the amazing diving opportunities.

In the late afternoons we would all gather at the only bar on the beach swapping our sailing stories over a beer or two. This interaction was really enjoyable and it was pleasant being able to talk to people again, particularly with people who share common interests. It was also so nice to be able to talk to Marilyn again on Skype for long periods and catch up with all the news from home.

The small dusty sleepy town comprised of a single road with a scattering of shops selling some building hardware, groceries and general mechanise. Houses were dotted behind the town at the base of the mountain. The locals were friendly and spoke French, Patois and English.

The anchorage was typical Polynesian with crystal clear turquoise water fringed by a reef. Strong tidal currents would stream through the anchorage at times so it was essential that the anchor was well set. I was told about the occasional boat which had to be towed off the reef after dragging anchor. The colour of the water was a beautiful creamy blue green and all shades to a dark blue in deep water. This anchorage, or for that matter, all the ones on Hua Hine were unsafe in the advent of a cyclone hitting the island.

After a couple of days I moved Grace to the more protected, calmer anchorage at Haavai Bay so that I could do a little painting and maintenance on the outside of the hull.

On the 28th of November I sailed the boat to Raitea Island and anchored off Utoroa point in the afternoon after a very pleasant five hours sail across the calm waters.

I put down two anchors because of the strong currents but I was not happy at all in the 20 metres depth of the water. Fortunately, the holding was good, as often it is not, because of loose broken coral shale on the bottom which makes it difficult for the anchor to catch.

I walked to town the next day and on speaking to another yachtsman I found out that I could tie Grace alongside the very modern well-built town dock. It was free of charge and would give me access to the fuel dock, shops and water. So I immediately moved Grace from the anchorage to this location. It was such a luxury to walk on and off of the boat and I also took liberties by exercising Beebee in the town as there were no other dogs around. The town consisted of two rows of quite scruffy shops stretching over a distance of 200 metres.

That night I enjoyed a beer sitting outside the restaurant which was alongside Grace's dock. There I was entertained by an amazing group of male and female dancers performing with traditional drumming and singing. The dancing was quite spectacular, so unlike anything I had seen before. It was complicated and very dramatic, a truly wonderful visual show.

On the 5th December I sailed across to the island of Tahaa, which was close to Huahine within the same perimeter reef. The next 4 days I spent in the quiet protected anchorage called Hamene on Tahaa, which I had all to myself. There was a fairly well stocked shop in the pretty village which was very clean and within close walking distance from the dinghy dock. Beebee and I would walk to the shop every day for our fresh French bread and other groceries.

Verdant hills surround the beautiful anchorage which could offer shelter in the advent of a cyclone but like all these anchorages, the holding is questionable. I spent the next 3 days taking down the genoa and repairing it by gluing strips of reinforcing cloth on to the rotten fabric. This I hoped would extend the life of the sail but embarrassingly, this made it look like a patch work quilt!

We left our peaceful anchorage 5 days later and

sailed for Bora Bora, arriving there in the afternoon and anchoring off the town of Vaitape in 26 metres of water. The island is often reported to be the most beautiful in the world. Without a doubt it has amazing water in the lagoon and is very volcanic and rugged, so beauty it has, but I found it very commercial. It definitely did not have the onshore beauty that I had found in the Marquesas. Having said this, the very best sunset photographs that I took of Grace where here, with the spectacular volcanic mountains as the backdrop.

On the 17th December we left Bora Bora, feeling somewhat irritated that the French police would not give me a proper clearance document. They expected me to e-mail all the forms to Tahiti who would then e-mail the clearance document back again to me. I was surprised that the French police would not do this for me. Needless to say, I left without clearance but I had completed all the documents in their office.

Our next destination will be Pago Pago in American Somoa. Following this my intention will be to keep sailing north across the 10th parallel, where we will be out of the cyclone belt.

15

Bora Bora to Pago Pago

Sunday 18th December 2016 Day 2

Run 70 miles

08:00 hours S 15 56 W 152 33

wind light NE overcast

heading 310 magnetic at 3 knots

Bora Bora is now 57 miles behind us, having sailed all night in squally winds under a double reefed main. I am deliberately keeping our heading North of our track, so we are close hauled on a port tack. It is my intention to get out of the cyclone belt as a priority.

At noon we have covered 70 miles, which I am pleased with and I have decided to bear away to a new heading of 300 magnetic. We are now 1,030 miles from our destination, Pago Pago. The wind is light at 10 knots from the NE and the sea is pleasantly flat.

Monday 19th December 2016 Day 3

Run 80 miles

wind N-NW 10 knots sea slight sunny

heading 280 magnetic at 4 knots

Aries steered without hesitation all night at 3 knots and the weather during the night remaining squall free and the sea very flat. I slept well through the night, catching up on sleep and I awoke this morning feeling refreshed and happy to be back in our sailing routine. This gentle windward sail we are now enjoying is making this early part of the passage very pleasant.

The genoa, unsurprisingly has ripped again but I have managed to get it down and it is now in the cabin, so tomorrow will be a repair day.

Our noon to noon run is 80 miles and in these light windward sailing conditions, it is a very good run for Grace.

Tuesday 20th December 2016 Day 4

08:30 hours S 15 20 W 154 15

wind calm sea flat overcast

We lost the wind at 15:00 hours yesterday and drifted overnight and today we are still without wind and I have been obliged to run the engine all day.

25th December 2016 Day 9
Pago Pago 811 miles
S 13 34 W 156 45
wind 0-10 west sea flat sunny

Last night was cool and overcast but we were fortunate not to have any rain. Our sail for the previous five days has been nothing but rain squalls and calms, so our mileage has been a record low figure and what little distance we have achieved has been done by running the engine frugally during the day.

At 17:00 hours the breeze is now allowing me to make two knots on course for Pago Pago. A large one metre swell is running from the south, which tells me that a south east trade wind is blowing in the south somewhere and there might be a possibility of it reaching us, but alas, it seems that the closer we get to the equator, the weaker the winds become!

I do not have a chart for this part of the Pacific so I have constructed one to fill in the gap to Samoa. I did this by pricking through the grid lines from the Society Islands chart on to the back of an old chart and then re-calibrating it to our location.

It's Christmas day today! This is our second one away from home since leaving, and at this time it is difficult not to think of family and feel a little homesick. My Christmas dinner was just the normal boat food of crackers and tinned sardines!

BEYOND THE SUNSET

27th December 2016 Day 11
Run 67 miles
08:00 hours S 13 43 W 158 36
Pago Pago 704 miles
wind SE 10 knots sea light sunny warm

We enjoyed a pleasant gentle sail yesterday but the wind became much lighter during the night and we only managed steerage speed. Our noon run is pleasing at a modest 67 miles. I expressed my dislike for these Pacific winds in the log today, stating that it seems we only get one day in ten of good sailing, or even good weather.

Sunday 1st January 2017 Day 16
Pago Pago 413 miles
10:00 hours S 14 15 W 163 35
wind SE 10-15 knots sea slight overcast

Calms and strong squalls, with accompanying rain, often very heavy, characterised the weather for the past 4 days. In spite of this we have managed to cover 219 miles even though we did waste many hours drifting with no wind.

At 13:00 hours I write in the log that this is the first time that the wind is in the south east for over a week and at 17:00 hours I record that we are now sailing downwind at six knots which is such a change from the past week. This is why we go sailing!

I sent a message to Marilyn on the tracker saying

"*Happy new year to you and all. Very hard sail – heavy rain and light breezes. Thinking of you and family, lots of love, Malcolm.*"

The following day the wind kept up and strengthened to 20 knots driving Grace on at six knots over a rough sea with Aries steering well on a dead run and the sails set wing and wing. The noon run was 95 miles which I am very happy with and is a record for this leg. At 17:00 hours the wind dropped and we fell back to doing only three knots on a broad reach, but the result of the earlier 20 knot wind has now brought us to 290 miles from Pago Pago.

Tuesday 3rd January 2017 Day 18
08:00 hours S 14 44 W 166 18
wind E 0-10 sea 1 metre swell
rain and squalls
steering 300 magnetic (need 270 magnetic)

From midnight until dawn the squalls made sailing all but impossible and the day has proved to be not much better with light winds all day and slatting sails in the swell. Our run of 61 miles is quite surprising under these conditions.

That night we once again endured light winds with calms and Aries was unable to steer the boat in these fickle conditions, so we resorted to drifting at times. I wrote in the logbook that this must be one of the worst passages we have ever made. This is meant to be a trade wind route but the winds are much more like the doldrums, in fact I would say that this is very typical of the doldrums. On checking the weather maps, they state that the doldrums are just south of the equator at this time of the year, so from this I must conclude that the doldrums have moved 300 miles south of their normal position. If that is the situation, then that puts us in this belt, I never thought that a 10 days trip would take 21 days in a trade wind belt!

In the early hours of Friday morning, we were about 30 miles from Pago Pago so I stopped the boat and waited for dawn before approaching the island. It stood out tall. stark and verdant green in the early morning light. After navigating our way through the reefs via the well-marked channel, we motored into the harbour and were instructed by the harbour master to tie up at the customs dock.

Six officials from various departments boarded and searched the boat quite thoroughly but were nevertheless very friendly and polite.

Once the formalities were completed I motored Grace much further into the head of bay where the water was seven metres deep. I dropped the anchor close to two American boats which were rafted together. They were in very poor condition, slowly rotting away at anchor and when I spoke to the elderly owners, it was explained to me that they had been there some years and were quite happy to stay there for the foreseeable future and enjoy the beautiful surroundings. There was a McDonalds restaurant a close dinghy ride away, where they breakfasted almost on a daily basis.

The anchorage was surrounded by forested mountains and was very beautiful, an idyllic place, except for two things, one being the amount of trivial pollution in the water and in the town and the other was the fish canning factory nearby, which filled the bay with an unpleasant smell when the wind blew from the wrong direction.

I had come here to stock up with food and diesel as I had heard that prices for these items here in Samoa were the cheapest in this part of the Pacific. They were cheaper, most definitely, but not as cheap as I had hoped and the charges to clear in and out were surprisingly high. However, I did find an excellent Chinese self-service laundry located on the roadside 100 metres form where Grace was anchored. It had modern machines and was the cheapest that I had ever come across at two dollars a load. They also offered a quality free internet service, which I took advantage of by calling Marilyn frequently. You could watch continuous American movies on a very large television screen whilst your laundry was being done. The only other internet service was in town and charged $5 for thirty minutes.

Even though Beebee was not allowed ashore, there was a field very close by which was always deserted, so I would take her there every day for a run and then she would swim back to the boat whilst I rowed the dinghy, this she loved.

The island also offered quite good repair facilities from small workshops located in an industrial area, a dollar bus ride away. I was fortunate in finding someone here to make new Aries brackets for me at a very reasonable price and he also gave me a couple of charts which I was missing.

I made friends with an American fellow called Tod, who was working on new tug boat which had recently arrived in the port for the island government. Tod was on a short term contract before soon returning to the States. He was obviously lonely and was anxious for non-island company, so as we could both talk about nautical matters, we immediately became friends. We had a good time together and he showed great interest in my circumnavigation and wanted to know as much as possible, as it was something he was keen on doing himself. His company and conversation I found very enjoyable and it was then that I realised how lonely I was as well.

On the 21st January we motored out of the harbour feeling sad at leaving my newly made friend, but anxious to leave the cyclone belt as the season was very much upon us now. The food lockers were now full again, most of it I bought from the Chinese supermarkets who were much cheaper than the American ones, as long as one was not too fussy. I also had refilled the diesel fuel tanks and so I left feeling that we were definitely well prepared for our long sail to the Solomon Islands.

16

Voyage to the Solomon Islands

We managed to maintain steerage all night on a gentle westerly wind towards West Samoa, intending to pass close without stopping. The island became visible on the port side in the afternoon about 15 miles away but I was pleased to sail on, heading almost due north as it was my intention to make as much northing as possible before turning for the Solomons. The cyclone belt generally does not extend past the 7 degree south parallel and here we should be out of the danger area, so I will use diesel to get us there as soon as possible.

On our second day at sea I record that doldrum conditions are persisting and both Beebee and I are feeling the heat with little or no breeze to give us some relief. The wind did return that evening giving Aries enough wind to steer the boat through the night but morning found us once again running the engine. Our noon run is a pleasing 103 miles due to our overnight sailing, had the wind remained calm, we would have drifted.

We will soon be crossing the 10th parallel which means the cyclone risk will become very much reduced and once we arrive at the 7th parallel we should be free of cyclones, but exceptions do happen! That evening I record in the logbook that the squalls have returned, accompanied by a breeze so I have set up Grace to sail on a close-hauled heading of 330 magnetic. This is not my preferred heading but it does take advantage of the light wind and is preferable to drifting. Although this heading does give us mileage gain towards the Solomon Islands, I would prefer to keep on pushing north for the 7th parallel.

Wednesday 25th January 2017 Day 4
S 10 09 W 172 25
wind 20-30 knots N-NW sea rough heavy rain
double reefed heading 020 N-NE

We have been hove-to for 6 hours today and most of the night, due to a constant changing squally wind. This situation developed during the evening yesterday and has persisted ever since. At 16:00 hours the squalls ease and I was able to re-set Grace sailing again. Due to the wind swinging into the north, I am obliged to head east of north which means we are sailing away from our gain to the west, so we are effectively sailing away from the Solomon Islands. This I have to accept, because the alternative would be south west and as I want north, I have to be content with this heading.

Furthermore, we seem to have bilge pump problems and the engine fails to start. To make matters worse, when I gibed the boat, the preventer managed to catch itself around a stanchion and ripped it out of the deck, causing a deluge of water on to the chart table, wetting the instruments and the logbook. I had just recently repaired a stubborn leak there! Adding to my woes, I discovered that a porthole in the forward cabin had burst open drenching everything, before I was able to attend to it. Fortunately, all the food stored there was double bagged in plastic so we suffered no loss to our stocks, but charts and books got a soaking!

The wind began to drop overnight and by the morning it was back to 10-15 SW allowing us to head almost due west and as we have now crossed the 10th parallel the cyclone hazard is at least halved in comparison to previously. I have fixed a temporary repair to the stanchion and hopefully this will stop the waterfall at the chart table.

Aries managed to steer throughout the night in the 25 knots of wind under a double reefered sail plan maintaining a fair speed. The bilge pump seems to be pumping a lot more than normal, which is very worrying as it is automatic, meaning that it switches itself on when the water reaches a certain level in the bilge. This frequent pumping means a lot more water is entering the boat than it should.

At 16:30 hours we are passing the island of Kezau, about two miles away on our port side. The wind has dropped down to 8-10 knots and the sea has become much calmer as well so I took this opportunity to try and start the engine, which had proved difficult recently. This I managed to do, so I have kept it running for four hours to re-charge the batteries. Our afternoon sail, dare I say it has become quite pleasant and I have also used this improving weather to try to dry books and charts from our deluge.

On Friday the weather remained warm and sunny with a steady 15 knot wind from the north east giving us a welcome five knots. The run for the last 24 hours is 98 miles which is pleasing and I believe anything near the magic 100, is always a bonus. At 17:30 hours the wind started dropping and at 19:00 hours it became necessary to start the engine but a little later, a gentle breeze encouraged me to switch off the engine, set Aries and go to sleep, leaving the boat and Aries to fend for themselves.

Saturday 28th January Day 7
Run 90 miles
08:00 hours S 07 53 W 174 15
wind light NE sunny sea flat hot

Grace steered through the night at a speed of 1-2 knots, unattended which was very pleasing and we also made 40 miles. This is a surprisingly good run for such light winds so I believe that whilst I slept the wind must have freshened.

I spent the afternoon repairing the coupling to the Aries rudder, from spares that I carried on board. Our noon run is very satisfying, but I must not forget that a lot of it was done on the engine the previous day.

At 21:00 hours a slight breeze has arrived which is

a change from our windless day allowing me to set Aries
and go to sleep.

Once again we did good mileage overnight enjoying
a very quiet peaceful sail, gliding along on a flat sea at 2
knots under an amazing star canopy. This allowed me a
good sleep and I only needed to come on deck three times
the whole night. Sunday morning brings us an 8 to 10
knot north east wind but it is overcast and squally, never
the less we are making 4 knots.

At 16:00 hours in the afternoon a pod of about a
dozen dolphins which were the large variety arrived and
swam around the boat for 2 hours. These were unusually
big mammals, quite unlike their smaller cousin, the bottle
nose dolphin. They were very vocal, emitting loud
squeaking sounds which could be heard clearly down
below in the cabin. I was concerned about them damaging
the Aries paddle which is quite fragile. For this reason I
motored away from them and then drifted but to no avail
they stayed beside us even when we were stationary. This
has never happened to me before but needless to say this
kept Beebee prancing around the deck for the duration.

Monday 30th January 2017 Day 9
Run 71 miles
07:30 hours S 07 57 W 176 55
wind 5/10 NE sea swell light cloudy
heading 270 magnetic at 4 knots

Aries steered the boat through the night in the

light winds and our noon run was 71 miles for the 24 hours, which I am not complaining about as I need to remind myself that we are sailing in the doldrum belt.

At 14:00 hours we are motoring as the wind once again has eluded us, but I am having trouble with Ray, the electric auto-pilot which has started switching itself off causing us to motor in circles. I have had to disconnect it and allow the boat to drift until the wind returns.

Returning to yesterday's Dolphin experience, I feel on reflection that this was an unusually profound occurrence. It has occurred to me that they stayed with Grace to befriend, help or defend us as the loud and continuous squeaking sounded anxious and concerned. At no time were they being playful which is the normal behaviour of prancing dolphins in the bow wave. When I stopped Grace and we drifted, about five of them lay together alongside the cockpit on the surface of the sea, squeaking very loudly. This I have never experienced before in dozens of dolphin sightings in many oceans over the last 30 years. I have heard many times sailors saying that they were warned by dolphins of some imminent danger or peril.

The following morning, Tuesday our 10th day at sea was a repetition of yesterday, giving us a run of 72 miles.

Shortly after noon a band of heavy rain squalls moved in requiring me to put three reefs in the mainsail as at times the winds were nearly gale force. The sea quickly became rough so it was necessary to put Beebee down below for the rest of the day. I recorded in the logbook at 19:00 hours that we have endured very strong winds and heavy rain all afternoon, accompanied by big seas.

Wednesday 1st February 2017 Day 11

Run 78 miles

wind NE 20/30 knots sea rough

cloudy and squalls

heading 270 magnetic at 5 knots

double reefed

My overnight sleep was interrupted because of a steady 25 knot wind accompanied by frequent strong near gale force squalls and big seas. This made it difficult for Aries to hold course requiring me to put on my oil skins and go on deck and re-set it frequently. Fortunately, the weather this morning has improved but we are still experiencing strong squalls and heavy rain. We have done a 75 mile run from noon to noon which is very acceptable in these very trying conditions.

At 17:30 hours in the afternoon the wind was still blowing at 15-25 knots, when we were hit by a very violent rain storm, knocking Grace on to her beam ends. Once she had righted herself I set her up in the heave-to position deciding to wait for these strong squalls to pass through. The winds remained very strong, almost gale force for the next two hours. Unfortunately, once again my well used genoa was blown out and it is now of no use whatsoever, until repaired.

We have just crossed the 180 degrees meridian and so we are in the Eastern half of the globe and because the date line runs approximately on this meridian we will be gaining a day.

Thursday 2nd February 2017 Day 12
Run 81 miles
07:30 hours S 07 58 E 179 14
wind N E 10/20 sea moderating
2 metre swell
Sunny heading 230 magnetic

I cannot decide whether or not to stop at Funafuti Island. The reef entrance will be rough in this weather and I really do not like atolls, with their coral heads and fast currents. I am making an approach but I may change my mind, although it will be far easier to make the repairs that Grace requires in a calm anchorage but the thought of the bureaucracy does put me off. Even though I am concerned at the weakness in my battery system which makes starting the engine difficult. But on second thoughts I have concluded that because one pair of batteries of the four on board are still in good condition, I can still maintain the bilge pumps and start the engine. For this reason I will carry on and do the necessary repairs in the Solomon Islands, even though I do not have the assurance of the second back up pair of batteries.

On the 3rd February which is our 13th day at sea after leaving Samoa, heading for the Solomons. The wind is north east and we are sailing under full mainsail over a moderate swell and the day remains warm and cloudy. Even though our overnight winds were light, Aries managed to steer the boat and we covered another 32 miles but just before dawn the Aries coupling broke again, so Grace turned herself around and we sailed backwards for a few miles before I woke up.

I spent the early morning repairing the coupling and by mid-morning we were once again sailing under full mainsail at four knots on course for the Solomon Islands. At noon I recorded a run of 68 miles which I am not overjoyed about but nevertheless every mile counts.

During the afternoon we crossed the 8 degree parallel and the wind became north east 10-15 knots so we were able to make 5 knots on the still quite rough seas. We are, of course sailing without our genoa which requires serious repair work, so my small staysail is having to fill in for the genoa.

Funafuti is now behind us and I have no regrets about not stopping and as we press on to the Solomons, I realise that I am so much happier passage making even with the re-occurring problems.

Saturday 4th February 2017 Day 14
Run 112 miles
09:00 S 07 56 E 176 18
wind N E 15/25 knots sea rough sunny
heading 270 magnetic at 6 knots

The wind kept up, growing stronger overnight giving us a really good 24 hour run of 112 miles, all done without the genoa.

The clouds are typical small puffy white trade wind clouds and the wind is north east. Now, the north east trades blow in the northern hemisphere, that is north of the equator, so I must conclude that they have crossed south of the equator and pushed the I.T.C.Z (doldrums) further south, which has been our experience. This north east wind has been blowing continuously for four days but not as fresh as today.

It is strange that I am no longer concerned about how many days we have sailed without a land fall, or for how many days we must still sail before we drop the anchor. It seems that I am quite content with this ocean routine.

The following morning I record in the log that the north east wind is remaining with us, giving Grace another good run of 112 miles again from noon yesterday.

Late in the afternoon we were visited by a pod of bottle nose dolphins which Beebee detected before they arrived around the boat, so it seems she could smell their fishy breaths when they were a long way off!

I have been studying the charts for the Solomons and have made the decision to land fall at Buala on the island of Isabel, which is now only 750 miles away.

Monday 6th February 2017 Day 16
Run 100 miles
09:00 hours S 07 36 E 174 25
Isabella 717 miles
wind NE 15-20 knots sea rough sunny
heading 290 magnetic making 5-6 knots

Every day that we have this wonderful north east wind is such a blessing, but strictly speaking this is a northern hemisphere trade wind, poaching in the southern hemisphere and I believe that the doldrums lie about two hundred miles to our south. Our overnight run puts us about 30 miles north of yesterday's position which means we are now well out of the cyclone belt, nevertheless I don't really want any more northing.

The evening brought a drop in the wind down to 10-15 knots, with much smaller seas, so I used this opportunity to take the genoa down below for repairs. This sail has been out of action for the past five days but I really do need it for down-wind sailing as the staysail is just a little bit too small for this point of sail.

Just before dusk I set Grace on a dead run using the staysail on a pole, which suits Aries quite well as it holds the boat on course without fuss.

Light winds overnight allowed us to make steerage

only, so our noon run has dropped in comparison to previous days. Regrettably I did not sleep well because Grace rolled a lot which was caused by the swell on the beam and the wind on the stern, always an uncomfortable combination in light winds. Besides that, it was a beautiful night, with almost a full moon, very little cloud and quite squall free.

The next day, our 17th at sea the wind remained light at 5-10 from the north, so it became necessary to start the engine, which I did with some trepidation, but it cranked strongly on the forward batteries and so we were able to motor until15:00 hours. At this time, the electric pilot Ray, stopped working, leaving me no choice but to allow the boat to drift until 20:00 hours, when a light breeze returned giving us enough speed to maintain steerage through the night, so Grace gently sailed on whilst I slept.

Wednesday 8th February 2017 Day 18
Run 75 miles
08:00 hours S 06 30 E 170 18
Isabel 646 miles
wind NE 10 knots sea slight sunny
heading 270 magnetic at 5 knots

Aries steered us through the night in the light wind but at the very least we kept sailing. I had spent yesterday gluing strips of cloth on to my very shredded genoa, which is really quite rotten, but today it is back in service, having re-fitted it in the light winds this morning. We did need a calm day to get the genoa back on without it flogging itself to bits, which it would do in any sort of wind. So, from this aspect the weather was kind to us. Once a sail is up and set tight in a wind, under working conditions, it is reasonably safe from damage but it is the violent flogging which is so destructive, particularly to old sails.

Grace is now sailing well, I believe her performance is really not too bad considering she is carrying small sails. Her motion is comfortable and I am sure that the new mast and rigging is under stressed, which gives me peace of mind.

At 18:00 hours I record in the logbook that the wind has eased to 10 knots and we are enjoying a pleasant afternoon sail in perfect weather. Grace has also managed to keep up a good five knot speed all day, with very little from me.

Overnight the wind became a little fresher, so we were able to keep going at five knots resulting in a good run of 126 miles for our noon position on Thursday the 9th of February. It seems that as long as we stay north of the 7 degree parallel we may continue to enjoy these wonderful north east winds.

I am an habitual book reader and love to spend 4 to 6 hours every day reading from a wide selection of the 300 books on board. I have previously read and will continue to read books by Patrick O Brian, who is one of my favourite authors, writing fiction set in the 18th century on Royal Navy frigates, during the Napoleonic Wars. I am now on a third reading of his twenty books and I continue to find delightful details in his writing that I had previously missed. His books were written with great integrity, enormous accuracy of the period and a well-researched understanding of the seamens' lot on a man of war at that time!

Unfortunately, the north east trade winds deserted us for the next seven days, leaving us once again at the mercy of the frustrating doldrums which were quick to take their place. I believe the trades moved north back over the equator to their normal tramping grounds.

The doldrums brought back to us` calm conditions, with their sudden changes to ferocious near gale force winds, forcing me to keep the sails reefed for most of the time and the remaining period drifting or motoring in the calms. The seas never had a chance to calm down so most days we were always uncomfortable. Heavy equatorial rain would accompany these squalls, so the boat was miserably damp and hot below decks. It was difficult to relax as I would be frequently up on deck, day and night tending to Aries and the sails. In spite of all this hard work with little peace, our mileages remained at a depressing average of fifty miles a day.

Friday 16th February 2017 Day 27
06:30 hours S 07 51 E 160 08
Isabel 37 miles
very light N wind sunny sea flat motoring

My great fear was to arrive off Bualo late in the afternoon or at sunset, thus making the reef invisible, which would result in having to wait off until mid-morning the next day before I could make passage past the reef. So it was fortuitous that a slight breeze kept us steering throughout the night, giving us a bonus run of 25 miles which was so amazing, leaving us just 37 miles to the anchorage from our daylight position.

At 07:30 hours the island became visible at 29 miles, so there seems no reason why we should not be in the anchorage by 13:00 hours by running the engine.

I am really looking forward to this landfall and the timing should make the reef very visible with the sun high. We have been 26 days at sea without a break, so it is high time for a change and I am quite sure Beebee would really enjoy some shore time!

The island became sharply visible at noon, high and volcanic, cloaked in dark green tropical rain forest from shoreline to the mountain tops which were hidden in the clouds. There was no sign whatsoever of any human corruption to this beautiful island from a distance and I am sure this is how it must have looked to the first explorers who laid eyes on it.

I passed the reef on my port side, which I could

only see because the water colour changed from a pale blue to an ominous brown colour. Because of the calm sea, there was no breaking waves on it to warn an unwary sailor of the hazard, so the high sun was a piece of good luck. A low sun angle as in the morning or afternoon, would make the reef quite invisible below the water because of reflection.

We motored across the beautiful aquamarine coloured lagoon to the small village, a cluster of timber buildings set behind a thin line of mangrove trees amongst which lay half a dozen dugout canoes. There was no dock or any sign of development, that one would expect in the main town of Isabel, we were definitely the only boat here except for the canoes!

After dropping anchor in five metres of water in front of the village I proceeded with my documents immediately to the police station, by walking on foot paths through the trees, which was shown to me by the helpful villagers who all spoke good English. This building was a modest single story brick building with a flag on a pole in front of it. The police were friendly and polite but insisted that I must sail as soon as possible to Honiara, the capital on the island of Guadalcanal and process my arrival there.

I remained at anchor for the next four days but the tiny village offered very little in the way of supplies, but I was able to get 50 litres of diesel from a man who sold it from drums. I world not normally buy from a drum, but beggars can't be choosers and I did discover that in most of the Solomon Islands, this was quite normal. This town

was definitely the most primitive that I have come across
in my travels and had no facilities such as cash machines
or internet. The only road was a gravel track barely 200
metres long. Notwithstanding all this the setting was
simply beautiful with the high rainforest covered mountain
immediately behind the village.

My most enjoyable experience was meeting
Dudley, a quietly spoken intelligent man educated in
America, the grandson of a Bishop Dudley who had been
knighted for his services to the Isabel community. Dudley
took me to see his grandfather's grave, which was an
elaborate marble construction in its own building,
beautifully engraved with the letters K.O.B.E. It was quite
obvious that the island held this man in very high esteem!

Dudley kindly invited me to his home to meet his
wife and children and have supper with them which
proved to be a very pleasant experience. His home was by
most standards a very modest affair, but was brick built
unlike most which were built of timber and placed very
close to one another. There were no cars in the village so
there were no roads that I could describe as such, but
plenty of foot paths. I did feel that there had been little
change to the islanders' way of life since the war but I
could be quite wrong as I spent so little time there.

The dug-out canoes now had outboard motors on
the back and some of them were made of fibre-glass, were
longer, wider and a lot more seaworthy than the traditional
boats. These modern canoes could travel to Honiara in a
day, or less, travelling at high speed across the various

lagoons between the islands at high speed loaded to the gunnel's with passengers and cargo.

The island was a mountainous rain forest, still unspoilt but I was told of an exclusive holiday resort 30 miles further up the coast, only accessible by boat which catered for the rich and famous. This island apparently was visited quite infrequently by yachts and Grace was only the second visiting yacht in the previous two years, but most of the other islands were more popular amongst the foreign yachts.

I have failed to mention to my reader that I did have an ulterior motive for including the Solomon Islands in my circumnavigation, so this is my reason.

When I was a child, my mother would frequently talk of her childhood in the Solomon Islands when she was about six years old.

My mother and her siblings lived on the island of Malaita, from where my grandfather ran a schooner, collecting copra from the various islands and then sailing the cargo to Australia where it was sold. My grandmother was an Australian doctor, who administered to the islanders, and at that time it was unusual for a lady doctor to be treating and working with the locals.

The name of the schooner was also Malaita and my mother would always speak fondly of it, particularly when discussing the native rebellion. Apparently, the family's cook, who was an islander, warned the family of a pending attack from the hill people, who some thought might still practise cannibalism. My grandfather quickly herded everyone including the cook, onto the schooner which was fortunately anchored in the bay, and immediately set sail for Australia, not returning until peace was restored. This I believe was done by the arrival of a gunboat and whether or not this account is true, I can't be sure but it does smack of British gunboat policy, which was often the way things of this nature were handled shortly after the Great War.

My mother would have loved to know of my Solomon Island stopover but alas, she passed away a few years before I started this circumnavigation.

On the 24th February we left for Honiara on the island of Guadalcanal, which is the main town in the Solomons.

At 21:00 hours I was forced to heave-to behind Florida Island because of strong squalls and remained there until 02:00 hours. Then the wind allowed me to continue sailing and at dawn we sailed through Sandfly Passage across the straights to Guadalcanal in very rough seas. On arrival at Honiara, the capital of the Solomon Islands, I attempted to anchor Grace amongst other yachts in the designated anchorage which was very rough. I soon realised that this anchorage was unsafe in these conditions so I moved Grace into the shipping harbour, a short distance away which offered more protection from the rough swell. By the following morning the weather had improved enormously and the dangerous swell was gone so I moved Grace back to the designated anchorage.

Honiara is a bustling busy town, very crowded,

scruffy with litter everywhere. However, the yacht club offered free facilities including showers and cheap beer! I soon got to know some long term Australian yachtsman and another solo circumnavigator who was French. He very kindly helped me to get my cruising permit online for Indonesia, which required computer skills beyond my limited ability. Photos, forms and boat paperwork had to be photographed, scanned and emailed to the Indonesian authorities. While I was in Honiara I also obtained a visitor's visa from the Papua New Guinea consulate in town. One thing which soured my stay here, was the fact that I had to pay 200 dollars for navigation light maintenance to the customs office. This was an iniquitous charge, as there are very few lights that I saw, or if they were there they failed to work.

Surprisingly almost everything was available in this large sprawling town and I was able to replace my gas cylinder and regulator for the cooker from a well-equipped hardware shop. Fresh fruit and vegetables were plentiful at the crowded local market and I was able to find a fair range of canned goods from the supermarkets.

Solomon Islands market

We left Honiara at 14:00 hours on Saturday 4th March and set off for New Georgia Island, enjoying a sunny clear afternoon motor sail in light winds. I was kept busy over night with the return of rain squalls in between very light winds whilst maintaining a look out for towed barges ferrying lumber from the nearby islands to the sawmills in Honiara. Grace sailed at 2 knots on a flat sea under an overcast sky, passing Russell Island in the early morning on Sunday. That night the wind remained light and Aries was able to steer our course.

Monday 6th March was a lovely sunny day with steady light winds which kept us sailing at 2-3 knots all day long over a very comfortable flat sea. I took this opportunity to climb up the mast to the spreaders and from this perspective take some video footage of Grace under full sail with the various islands forming the backdrop. I really enjoyed this magical experience perched up on the mast looking down on Grace with her sails full and drawing without any flutter sailing quietly over this beautiful gentle blue sea.

That night the breeze became lighter but we still managed to keep sailing at 1.5 knots on a very calm flat sea, under an amazing spread of stars which were reflected in the mirror like water.

Tuesday morning found us 6 miles from Lever Harbour on New Georgia Island. We motored through the Gulf of Kula, which was a narrow, windy and quite beautiful passage, with the rain forest on both sides. I anchored Grace in mid-afternoon south of Nora in the lagoon amongst a host of little islands in 3 metres of water and there we remained for the night.

The following day I motored to Gizo through the beautiful Vonavana Lagoon. These lagoons amongst the islands and reefs are a very enchanting turquoise colour due to the limestone and coral and are quite unlike anything I have ever seen. I anchored Grace in 3 metres of water in front of tatty waterfront shops, bars and businesses.

Gizo town, on Gizo Island is populated with mixed European Polynesian and Melanesian races but all the businesses and infrastructure seem to be run by Chinese immigrants and this has created some resentment between them and the indigenous people. To this end on some of the islands, Chinese people were made very unwelcome and discouraged from opening businesses. In some ways this was to the detriment of the community because the Chinese brought their business skills and hardworking ethos to the islands. It was really a quaint back water place but surprisingly most things could be bought or ordered in from the Capital. The well run hospital provided inexpensive anti malaria drugs and the bank had a good working cash machine unlike some other islands where I had to tramp far and wide to find a cash machine with money in. The market sold a wide array of tropical fruit and a huge abundance of inexpensive fresh fish such as a 50 kilo tuna or a 1 kilo fish. The stalls displaying the produce were a rough collection of crude plywood structures or in some cases just selling off of the ground, all crammed closely together under ragged plastic tarpaulins. The whole area was very crowded with jostling colourful people who were cheerful and always very friendly.

I bought my food stocks from the Chinese stores which were surprisingly inexpensive but the variety was limited. There were two waterfront bars, a short row in my dinghy from Grace which was anchored out in the charming lagoon. I soon made friends with the sailors on three other yachts who were anchored near me in the lagoon.

The modern post office provided a very good internet service in two small private rooms with computers, desks and chairs, so I was able to speak with

Marilyn almost on a daily basis. The anchorage was very picturesque with small islands dotted about, on some of which were built very simple homes, often on stilts on the water. Pulled up on their little beaches would be the family dugout canoes and splashing around in the shallow water were children playing. On a daily basis a very narrow canoe would pass close to Grace on its way to the market with the family, grandma in the back then came the daughter and the two grandchildren in the front. We would exchange greetings and smiles, they being very intrigued by the strange presence of a dog on a boat. Beebee kept all unwanted visitors and canoes at a distance when I was not on the boat, which I did not discourage as petty pilfering from visiting yachts was not entirely unheard of. I was able to land Beebee frequently for walks even though strictly speaking this was not allowed. I would exercise her on a daily basis by allowing her to swim behind the dinghy as I rowed up and down the lagoon, which she loved.

The only unpleasant thing to cloud the sky was the recent drowning of a young lady off a German yacht during a diving accident. However, the other yachties who were there at the time were all adamant that this was no accident but believed that this was a murder, as an excessive amount of lead weights were found in her diving wet suit. The police had withheld his passport and so he was unable to leave whilst I was there.

I stayed in the anchorage at Gizo until Thursday 6th April, leaving at 09:00 hours, heading back to Nora to buy duty free diesel and obtain my outward clearance from the Solomon Islands.

Shortly after picking up the anchor, I promptly ran into the reef, which I could not see in the bad light on this grey day! The bilge pumps immediately started to run, and on inspection of the bilges, found that I had cracked the garboard plank on the port side.

After checking the damage from the inside of the boat, I made the decision to carry on to Nora. Once we were out of the reef area and back in deep water, I caulked the cracks from the inside of the boat by hammering in strips of cotton into the cracks using a screwdriver and I was relieved to see that I was able to stop most of the leaks.

We entered the entrance to the lagoon at Nora at mid-afternoon, which was marked by a single stick and proceeded close up to the shore where I dropped the anchor in clear water. I dived down to check the damage and found that it was not too bad and would allow me to keep sailing until I could find a facility where I could haul Grace and make proper repairs.

Nora was a small muddy not very clean village but the people were friendly and helpful and it was a simple matter to arrange the documentation for the purchase of duty-free diesel from the commercial dock. This could only be done after clearing out formalities were completed the following morning. This all went without any problems and the men at the dock pumped the fuel into Grace in a most friendly and courteous manner.

17

Nora to Papua New Guinea

Friday 7th April 2017 Day 1

After taking on diesel we left Nora heading through the lagoons on a hot and sunny afternoon towards Messina Island which is part of Papua New Guinea. The wind was very light south west so we were forced to motor across the very flat water.

I felt that the Solomons had been the most enjoyable island group that I had visited to date, putting this down to amongst other things, the friends that I had made. There was always at least five yachts anchored at Gizo and we all met regularly at the P T 109 Bar for a sociable visit which was very enjoyable, being able to talk about our similar experiences. Two friends, Fritz and Linder were on a New Zealand boat and Masa, an Australian single hander stand out in my memory. Masa took me across the reef one night to a bar on a resort island and needless to say, our drunken high speed return in the moonlight across the reef was an unforgettable dinghy ride. Masa never did things by half!

Saturday 8th April 2017 Day 2

Run 95 miles

08:00 hours S 08 53 E 156 24

wind 0-15 N overcast with rain squalls

At 08:00 hours I logged a run of 65 miles since leaving Nora due in main to a steady breeze through the night and surprisingly the rain and squalls did not deter Grace from keeping up a steady pace. I suffer the normal depression whenever we leave, especially after a long break and I put this down to the return of loneliness, plus the anxiety during the first day or two until we re-establish our routines. But today I am happy to be back at sea even though I will be trying for a nonstop sail through the Torres Straights to Indonesia which will be at least 25 days.

We maintained steerage speed through the night and fortunately the 8 to 10 knot breeze continued on Sunday morning. I have set up a weigh point at Messina Island as our heading, which is 155 miles away across the Solomon Sea. The day became hot and sunny and the early morning squalls disappeared but alas so did the wind obliging me to run the engine. Our run of 75 miles is about par for the conditions.

Monday 10th April 2017 Day 4
Run 80 miles
08:00 hours S 10 04 E 154 02
Weigh point Messina 100 miles
wind 10–15 knots N overcast sea slight
heading 240 magnetic at 5 knots

I woke up to a fresh breeze driving Grace at an efficient 5 knots after a gentle overnight sail in perfect tranquillity. It always amazes me that after a windless day, spending most of the time motoring at 800 r.p.m., we get a breeze which allows Aries to steer us at 2 to 3 knots through the night. This seems to happen most nights and a run of 80 miles is quite pleasing under these circumstances.

Tuesday 11th April 2017 Day 5
Run 75 miles
Noon S 10 34 E 152 42

Noon found us motoring along the north side of Messina island in heavy windless rain at 4 knots. I had considered a stop over here but changed my mind, even though I have the requisite visa. During the afternoon the wind swung to the west, which brought it directly on to the nose leaving us no choice but to punch against the sea chop at a very slow 1.5 knots because of an opposing current. Unfortunately, I cannot change course as we have to clear Deboyne Island before we can swing south towards the Conflict Islands Group

On Wednesday morning the wind dropped back to almost calm and we are now motoring south to the Conflict Islands. All the previous night I had to frequently plot our position on the chart, keeping alert to current drift whilst sailing hard on the wind due West, the only heading that we could make. This is very tiring, as this area demands careful navigation. For once in my life I have excellent paper charts of the whole area which were given to me by a couple from a yacht called Ondine.

This whole area is very shallow so it requires a careful watch on our position and on the depth sounder. That night required vigilant navigation once again and I continued to run the engine which I would not normally do but did so as sleep was not on the menu because of ever present dangers. Although it remained windless, the sea surface was all a flutter caused by the currents which at 2 to 3 knots can drive an unwary yacht quickly into invisible dangers below the surface.

A bright moon was a very welcome companion in helping me to see the many small islands in this very shallow challenging area.

This area was also devoid of any sign of visible humanity and I failed to see any ships or boats at all, during the crossing of the Coral Sea.

Thursday 13th April 2017 Day 7
Run 70 miles
09:00 hours S 11 00 E 150 48
wind calm hot and sunny drifting

At 03:00 hours we crossed over the Sunken
Barrier Reef into the Coral Sea, so now I would hopefully
be able to catch up on some lost sleep!

The logbook showed that at 09:00 hours we were
once again drifting on a very flat sea which is now the
Coral Sea and the water is very much deeper at around
2000 metres.

Late in the afternoon I discovered that the current
was drifting Grace back over to the Sunken Barrier Reef
due to a change in the tidal set, so we were going
backwards! One piece of good news was the discovery that
one of my diesel tanks which I had presumed empty, was
actually still half full, which now gives me the confidence
to carry on to the Torres Straights without a fuel stop, an
idea that had been lurking in the wings.

Friday morning saw us as usual running the
engine at idle speed on a windless flat sea, having once
again drifted all night. But that evening a very welcome
breeze arrived, which allowed us to sail on a broad reach
at 3 knots and at times Grace would push her speed up to
5 knots making an enjoyable change.

Saturday 15th April 2017 Day 9
Run 68 miles
08:00 hours S 11 00 W 149 33
wind E NE 0 to 10 knots overcast
heading 300 magnetic at 2 knots

I was a little disappointed with our noon run at 68 miles but I should not complain, as we have had the wind with us all day. Could this be the start of the famous Torres Straits trade winds which are reputed to be the most consistent trade winds of all, almost guaranteed to always blow.

Beebee's hair I have noticed, is growing quite fast since I gave her a haircut four days ago when it became apparent that she was really feeling the heat. Having a black coat and a long one at that, made her suffering worse. Her lovely shiny black coat looked as though she had been chewed by rats after I had cut it, definitely not an entrant to a beauty contest but her comfort really improved.

At 18:00 hours we are still sailing wing and wing downwind on course making a good 5 knots in the 12 to 15 knot wind.

Sunday morning's log entry stated that the wind had remained steady all night and Aries coped well giving us a good overnight run in spite of the sea becoming quite rough. The wind is still with us but rain accompanies it but by noon it became fresh at 15 to 20 knots requiring a reef. By 18:00 hours the wind was blowing at 30 knots

accompanied by heavy rain and rough seas so I set Grace
to heave-to in preparation for the night. Our noon run was
a satisfying 90 miles for Sunday.

On Monday morning, after remaining hove-to all
night, I managed to get Grace sailing again with two reefs
in the mainsail, on a heading of 260 magnetic making 5
knots. We had remained hove-to since 18:00 hours
yesterday, drifting in the current to lea, covering 17 miles.

Our noon run was poor at 32 miles mainly due to
our drifting overnight. I write in the log that I would like to
set more sail, but postpone it as we are surrounded by
heavy black squalls. My patience was rewarded and two
hours later the improving conditions allowed me to shake
out a reef.

Torres Straights are known for their strong,
continuous trade winds so it is quite possible that these
are the winds which we are now experiencing because we
are within 150 miles of the straights. Gizo in the Solomons
is 500 miles behind us and we are 1,500 miles from Timor
in Indonesia, which looks to me as a likely landfall. I
record in the log that I am looking forward to the Torres
Straights challenge, but not without some trepidation.

Tuesday 18th April 2017 Day 12

Run 93 miles

S 10 44 E 145 55

Unfortunately, I spoke too soon last night about
improving weather conditions, because by midnight the

wind was once again blowing near gale force in very strong squalls. We remained double reefed, heading 300 magnetic on a dead run.

Aries struggled to keep our course, so I was frequently up on deck getting Grace back on heading, from a wild dash to windward, caused by knock from a breaking sea. I read in the pilot book that these Torres Straights winds are trade winds, which are known at times to blow near gale force, for days on end.

At 08:00 hours we are sailing on a heading of 315 magnetic, which I need to hold so as to pass west of Eastern Fields Shoals to avoid its hazards.

Noon brought an easing of the winds and I recorded a very pleasing run of 93 miles. I am plotting our position every two hours so as to monitor our drift in the currents and to keep a check of our track on the chart.

These grey skies and a lack of sunlight have prevented my batteries from taking a full charge from the solar panels. This is disconcerting as my bilge pumps require a lot from the batteries particularly in rough weather.

During the afternoon and evening the rough seas continued to build and some huge waves were breaking on Eastern Fields reef. This general area approaching Torres Straights is very shallow being only 20 to 30 metres at its best which creates big breaking seas in bad weather.

Also present in the waves were huge floating logs, whole trees and lots of surface pollution drifting down from Papua New Guinea. This flotsam was becoming increasingly hard to see and avoid in the fading twilight. which posed a very serious hazard as a collision with one of the trees would be devastating!

Wednesday 19th April 2017 Day 13

Run 88 miles

08:00 hours S 09 37 E 145 03

wind SE 15-knots sunny sea rough big swell

heading 350 magnetic

The wind this morning has dropped to 15 knots but the sea remains rough but I expect it to begin improving soon.

At noon I gibed the boat on to a new heading of 280 degrees magnetic which would take us to Bramble Key, considered to be the start of the Torres Straights. As we approached Bramble Key, I wrote in the logbook that today has been a relaxing, enjoyable one in contrast to the previous days since leaving the Solomon Sea. This day has been one of those rare, perfect sailing days. At 18:00 hours we were now 40 miles from Bligh entrance light, the beginning of the marked passage through Torres Straights.

Thursday morning brought heavy rain and strong winds after an easy sail overnight. We struggled all morning in winds gusting to 35 knots, whilst heading SW down the Straights in difficult visibility due to the very heavy continuous rain. Our noon position put us off Warrior reefs, where upon we lost the wind, so I let Grace drift whilst I serviced the engine.

I realised that I did not have a chart for the second half of the Torres Straights, two copies of the first but none of the second so I spent time copying details from my Open C.P.N. computer chart which Fritz had downloaded for me in Gizo. I really blessed him for this kind act.

The wind and rain returned in the evening and we continued in foul weather towards Arden Island, plotting our position constantly as the strong currents were quick to put us out of the channel into dangerous shallow water, which had happened on two occasions!

On Friday morning the wind became stronger, requiring me to put in double reefs to the mainsail.

We sailed in poor visibility down the North East Channel past Coconut Island, Walker Shoal, Richardson Reef, Bett Island and navigated in the rain after sunset to Kirk Dale Reef. At midnight I snatched a one and a half hour sleep on the stretch to Edwards Rock, as I felt this area was relatively free of hazards should we drift out of the channel. I had previously identified this section as the only safe area where I could sleep. Anchoring behind islands or shoals in the whole of the Torres Straights area is considered very dangerous as the holding is always bad and the area is swept by very strong changing currents.

The weather throughout Friday remained poor with heavy rains and winds combined with very poor visibility. I recorded in the log *"Friday night until Saturday morning was one of the most frightening sailing nights I have ever experienced"*. With winds gusting to gale force, very heavy rain, big seas, treacherous cross currents, reefs all around within two to four miles most of the time and zero visibility. This required constant vigilance and plotting our position continuously as the cross currents were running up to four knots. The main was jammed in the second reef so I was unable to reduce it to the third reef. I was totally, mentally and physically exhausted but I could not enjoy the luxury of sleep!

Saturday 22nd April 2017 Day 16

09:00 hours S 08 E 142 27

wind very light rain showers overcast

We sailed past Wednesday and Hammond Islands to Goods Island where I anchored in a pretty bay in complete solitude at 11:30 hours.

I immediately took to my bunk and slept until late in the afternoon. The current was still against me so I decided to stay in the anchorage until the morning and carry out the work on the mainsail.

When I awoke after twelve hours of sleep, I felt totally refreshed and ready to carry on. The rain picked up overnight but we remained snug in the anchorage and quite safe in the light wind.

We left the Goods Island anchorage at 09:00 hours taking advantage of a favourable current stream which gave us a speed of 8-9 knots which was absolutely amazing as the engine was driving us at only 4 knots.

I sent a message to Marilyn via the satellite tracker, saying, "*Survived Torres gales rain rocks and reefs with treacherous currents and no sleep now onwards to Indonesia."*

At noon we came abreast of Booby Island light 3 miles away, which is the end of Torres Straights, I wrote in the log *"Never again!"* but having said that, in good weather with two extra crew members, the straights would not be nearly as challenging.

18

Across the Arafura Sea

Monday 24th April 2017 Day 18

Run 95 miles

07:00 hours S 07 E 140 41

wind E-SE 20-25 knots sea very rough overcast

running on 3 reefs at 5 knots

We are now in the Arafura Sea which shows little change from the previous days as the wind last night remained strong and the seas were very rough. I need one good day to replace the lines on the Aries (our wind pilot) which I noticed have become badly worn.

A peek of the sun from behind the low scudding black clouds is the first we have seen of the sun for many days.

Fortunately from early afternoon the wind began to drop and when I awoke at 17:00 hours, after 2 hours of afternoon sleep I was greatly relieved to see that the wind had abated and was now blowing a gentle 10 knots, the sea had also become much calmer, so I immediately shook out the reefs.

Tuesday's entry in the logbook at 08:00 hours states that the wind is once again blowing 20 knots South East and the sea has become rough again. This deterioration took place overnight from midnight and sleep became difficult after 03:00 hours. The swells were up to 3 metres making for a rough ride and this I put down to the relative shallow water in this area which is only 40 metres deep.

Our noon run is 86 miles which is good under the circumstances. At 13:00 hours we were struck by a very violent gale force squall which lasted one hour and by 17:00 hours we were totally becalmed on a very confused sea.

Wednesday 26th April 2017 Day 20

Run 60 miles

08:00 hours S 10 36 E 138 02

wind SE 5-10 knots sea flat some sun

heading 290 magnetic

Aries successfully steered us through the night from 21:00 hours when I turned off the engine. The night remained clear with no rain or squalls and we sailed under a starry canopy over a tranquil rested sea.

Once again I spent a lot of time replacing broken mainsail slides. The manufacturer used cheap plastic slides instead of nylon and furthermore they were spaced too far apart for the size of the sail. I did curse them loudly using all the foul words I had in my vocabulary. A lot of time has been spent during the last year working on the broken slides.

The day developed into a very enjoyable sailing day with abundance of sun putting a good charge into the

batteries. I took advantage of the good weather to once
again take down the genoa and glue on another dozen
patches to the rotting sail.

Patches !

At 19:00 hours I set up Grace under full main and
staysail for an optimistic night sail.

On Thursday morning I logged that the wind was SE at 10-20 knots with the return of squalls causing a 2 metre running sea.

Our run at noon was 82 miles which is an improvement, considering that I am nursing the sails as we still have a long way to go and their condition can be rated as poor to junk. Grace is now in need of general maintenance particularly the sails and all the sheets could do with replacing. Recently I have changed my approach in giving preference to the preservation of the equipment rather than pushing for speed.

Grace today is pushing ahead at a good downwind run doing 5 knots under a single reefed main, with the staysail boomed out on the pole, while the genoa remains in the cabin undergoing repairs. At 16:00 hours the wind freshened to 15-20 knots so I re-set Grace to a broad reach on a port tack which resulted in a brisk 6 knot reach.

On the 28th April I wrote in the logbook that this was our third week at sea without a land fall, disregarding the day anchored in Torres Straights. We could have stopped in Papua New Guinea, in the Louisiades or Port Moresby but the prime object of this trip is to circumnavigate Grace and not to tour or visit new places because this happens in due course without intention. Touring and visiting extends the trip and I really want to get home with Beebee and live in my house with its wild 2 acres garden and of course to be with Marilyn and friends and it would be so nice to spend Christmas in England with my children and grandchildren.

The next 7 days was spent crossing the Arafura Sea to Timor and went without any undue dramas. We experienced the normal light winds which are now predominant, the strong squalls of previous, with their 30 knot winds were thankfully now absent. However, our daily runs remained in the 70 to 100 miles range, making for a slow passage. The frequency of calms were high as this area is renowned for its light winds.

I did spend some time studying the charts for the Red Sea route back into the Mediterranean, which had been my original intention, as the piracy threat had diminished to almost zero.

Thus, with a little luck, I could be home by Christmas, keeping to my two year time frame which I had committed to Marilyn at the onset of the trip.

The other choice would be the long southern route around South Africa and then north up to the West Indies, followed by sailing on to Bermuda before turning east for Gibraltar. This is the classic route, which I have done twice from South Africa forty years ago, so I do not have a great yearning to do it again. Furthermore, my finances would not permit a further 12 months at sea, as this would be the case, before I arrive home. My remaining life I believe is too short to spend a year of it repeating what I had already done forty years ago. Also, Grace is not really up to it without a lot of repair and maintenance work done on her, a haul out, sail repairs and a new genoa.

Technically once I reach Durban in South Africa I

will have done a circumnavigation so I could end the trip there, but disposing of Grace and flying home is not acceptable at all. After all these years of trying for a solo circumnavigation, to take third prize by stepping off an aeroplane in Kefalonia has absolutely no appeal in comparison to stepping of Grace's deck in my home port in Greece.

Thursday 4th May 2017 Day 27
Run 67 miles
08:00 hours S 10 23 E 126 09

Squalls and calms are continuing today as they have for the previous three days which is really frustrating as we should have arrived in Timor by now. We have diesel remaining for 25 miles at 1,000 r p m or 35 miles at idle speed, we are 154 miles from Timor, so I really cannot use the engine, as I must keep what is left for making entry into Kupang.

Friday morning offered little change from the previous day and I awoke feeling tired from having to repeatedly get up and re-set Aries which did not seem to want to steer and I put this down to the fact that it really does need a good servicing and replacement of the lines. Also, the rudder cables to the main rudder have become very stretched and so also need tightening, so this is compounding the problem with Aries.

Friday's run was the same as yesterdays at 67 miles and at 18:00 hours we are now 52 miles from

Kupang. The afternoon sail was quite an amazing change with a perfect 12 knots breeze and a lovely clear cloudless sky.

I awoke on Saturday morning, our 30th day at sea, with the island of Timor just two miles away, we had done better speed overnight than I had anticipated, due most likely to a favourable current, so I was quite shocked to see the close proximity of land! Kupang did not offer any wonderful bays where I could anchor, so I chose to drop the hook close to fishing trawlers who were three abreast on what was obviously very limited docking space.

What I could see of the island was not overly attractive with no apparent beaches or dramatic landscape, unlike the Solomons. The area where the trawlers were tied up looked busy and bustling with people cars and unattractive buildings which serviced the fishing boats. Kupang, the city was behind the peninsular, so was not apparent from the anchorage.

As it was Saturday I made no attempt to go ashore, instead spent the rest of the day sleeping and relaxing. On Sunday I remained on board but did put up my yellow quarantine flag which meant under international maritime law that I had arrived from abroad and was requesting clearance, so basically the ball was in their court even though I did not think for one moment that the officials would come out to the boat. I spent the day replacing Aries lines and tensioning the rudder cables, as well as working on the sails. Maintenance work carried on through Monday and by the evening I was satisfied that

Grace was once again ship-shape and good for the next leg, only requiring fuel water and provisions.

On Tuesday morning I took Grace to the dock and tied up alongside a large wooden trawler. The crew on board were reasonably helpful and assisted me in this process. Within minutes a young man arrived on the dock on a small motorcycle and he was very quick to convince me to hire him to fetch diesel and water on his motorcycle. I gave him my containers and within two hours he had delivered 135 litres of diesel and 75 litres of water on board. I then rode on the back of his motorcycle to the immigration department to do all my clearance into Indonesia, followed by a 15 kilometres ride to the shops and supermarkets, where I stocked up on provisions and naturally not forgetting a litre of beer. I might add, that riding through town on the back of this motorcycle was not without a lot of excitement as my driver weaved through dozens of other motorcycles, which really proliferated the roads.

The town was full of small colourful shops, never exceeding two stories, the pavements were crowded with shoppers and workers and the streets were full of cars and motorbikes, a really populous place.

At 16:00 hours I moved Grace off the fishing trawler and returned to the anchorage. My Indonesian friend earned from me that day about 40 US dollars, so all in all he did well as the normal low wage earner would get only 100 dollars for a month's work.

19

The Indian Ocean to Bali

Wednesday 10th May 2017 Day 1

We left the anchorage at Kupang at 11:00 hours after completing the last of the repairs and refitting the Aries paddle.

I sailed Grace out through the inter-island currents and by mid-afternoon had cleared the coastline and we were back in open water. My log recording at 19:00 hours states that the South East wind is blowing at 20 knots and we are heading 270 magnetic, doing 5 knots. Grace is double reefed and the sea state moderately rough.

Through the night I was obliged to set the alarm clock for 45 minute intervals as the shipping traffic and trawler boats always seemed to be about. The sea state improved, the wind remained constant and Aries was steering well after the TLC given in Timor, all in all, a good first night.

I awoke at 09:30 on Thursday morning to see the large island of Seba on our port beam, just four miles away. This was a major navigation error because at 03:00 hours I had deduced that we would not arrive at Seba before late morning and we would be at least 10 miles off. So, I felt quite red faced, not to speak of the hazards of sleeping whilst the boat sailed so close to land. In hindsight I believe that there was a likely hood that I had picked up a very favourable current set.

Our noon run of 102 miles was quite satisfying for our first night out. We are enjoying a good running sail on a sunny trade wind sea, with the wind blowing at a steady 10 to 15 knots easterly.

Our heading will bring us quite close to the large island of South Sumba. At sunset I reset Grace on a broad reach to take account of the wind swing to South East and we are now getting wind squalls, which altogether signifies the arrival of a new weather system. By 20:00 hours the wind had picked up to 25 knots, requiring a double reefed main but Aries surprisingly held our course on a broad reach without too much bother.

Friday 12th May 2017 Day 3
Run 98 miles
09:00 hours S 10 35 E 120 12
wind 8-12 sea 1 metre swell sun and cloud

Sumba Island is visible on the starboard beam about 15 miles away and it is time now to jibe to 320 magnetic, our new heading, which is the course to Bali.

Our noon run is 98 miles and as I always say, anything around 100 miles a day is par for the course. At 19:30 hours I record that most of the day has been cloud free, the clearest sky we have seen in a long while. The wind has picked up to south east 20 knots, so I have rolled up the fragile genoa.

At midnight the wind eased, as had been the case for the previous two nights and shortly after sunrise on Sunday morning, our 4th day at sea, I was able once again to put the genoa to work on a south east 10 to 15 knot wind. The sky was overcast this morning and the sea is running a one metre swell.

Aries has really been steering Grace well on a dead run for most of the previous three days, since we entered the Indian Ocean, a first time for Grace.

We have now sailed more than three quarters of my circumnavigation, leaving behind in Grace's wake a very long furrow in the ocean.

At sunset the wind remains light at 10 to 12 knots, so I am also running the engine but surprisingly our speed is under 4 knots so from this I must conclude that we are fighting an opposing current of around 1 knot. We are now 196 miles from Bali and I am really looking forward to a break and some civilisation.

Sunday 14th May 2017 Day 5
Run 99 miles
07:30 hours S 09 39 E 117 20
wind very light 8 knots sea slight sailing at 4 knots

We made a steady 4 knots all night in a wonderful south east 10 knot wind without any squalls and Aries requiring no attention at all. It was a most enjoyable sail under a clear starry sky over a shiny calm sea. We are now 131 miles from Bali and I need to be sure at noon that we have less than 120 miles remaining to allow for a mid-afternoon arrival in Bali. To this end I will have to run the engine as well as keeping up full sails unless the wind freshens. At 19:00 hours we had only 81 miles remaining which is very pleasing and I believe we must be riding on a 1 knot current, such a bonus out of the blue.

On Monday morning only 43 miles remained and things looked good but by early afternoon we found ourselves in a 2 knot opposing current, which caused a very lumpy sea. Our forward speed over the ground dropped to 2 knots in spite of running the engine.

The city of Benoa was very obvious now with its abundance of tall buildings and the approach up the channel was filled with pleasure boats towing holiday makers on rafts or suspended from parachutes, criss crossing the channel, a far cry from the Solomon Islands. We were now approaching a very busy bustling city, bringing with it all the things I do not like about civilisation, pollution and crowds.

I was able to pick up a mooring near the yacht club, with guidance and help from a local man on an adjacent boat, and after a bucket wash took myself ashore to register my arrival at the club. This was done without any ceremony, I noticed that the marina had half a dozen Australian yachts, who I was told later were the front runners of a regatta from North West Australia which apparently is an annual event. All the facilities of the club including hot showers were made available free of charge and I anticipated a very pleasant stay here in Benoa.

Having Grace secure on a mooring, which cost me 5 dollars a day was a worry free relief, which gave me the peace of mind to enjoy my stay in Benoa. There was a recently arrived large American boat, also sailed single handed by a man called John Bouma. Because of his outgoing manner and hospitable attitude, we soon became friends.

The following morning he took me to the customs and immigration offices to complete my arrival formalities. John had done this four days previously when he arrived from Guam on his yacht 3/4 Time so he was very familiar with these routines and locations.

Because Beebee was not allowed off of the boat here, I decided from the onset to keep my stay short. My priorities were to take on diesel fuel, water, refill our larder as well as bringing my maintenance and sail repairs back to a workable level. Everything was available and could be ordered through the club. I took advantage of this and had 14 stainless steel slides made to order which cost me a hundred dollars, a very reasonable price for what turned out to be such a quality handmade job.

John and I shared taxis to travel around Benoa, seeing a bit of tourist stuff and seeking out supplies for our boats, like engine oil, filters, rigging bits and other necessary paraphernalia which is always required in replacing worn out equipment. We enjoyed each other's company, had lots of things of common interest to talk about and I would spend many an evening having a beer on his boat.

20

3,400 miles to Mauritius

On the morning of 24th May, I said a quick goodbye to Marilyn on Skype at the club, went on to say goodbye to John on 3/4 Time, who was also leaving and we had done our outward clearance together the day before.

　After re-stowing the dinghy on deck I dropped the mooring and motored from the club behind 3/4 Time which was thirty minutes ahead of Grace. I could see John's boat ahead of me, approximately 5 miles away. My heading was Mauritius, nonstop about 3,400 miles away, so this will be a long sail.

　The eight day stay in Bali had been very pleasant and I had an enjoyable social time because of John's company at the yacht club. During our frequent phone calls Marilyn had expressed to me her concern for me taking Grace through the Red Sea. My children Fiona and Neil had the same concerns and were quite sure that the piracy threat off the Somali Coast had not completely gone away.

　John had told me that it was his intention to take on a crew member in South Africa at Richards Bay, to accompany him down the 800 miles coast and around Cape Agulhas to Cape Town. This trip I had taken twice previously so I made the suggestion that if he were to make it worth my while financially, I would accompany him on his yacht. He took me up on this offer and agreed as well, to pay my travel expenses back to Richards Bay where I would leave Grace during the 10 day sail on ¾ Time. He also agreed to pay me half of the remuneration before we left Bali and the balance in Cape town.

This extra revenue is what made me finally change my mind from the Red Sea route and replace it with taking Grace around the Cape instead. It would help with the cost of hauling the boat in Richards Bay, the extra preparation required for a longer time at sea, as now I had extended my sail by six months. So, it is for this reason that we are now heading for Mauritius instead or a more northerly route to the Red Sea.

At sunset, I could just see 3/4 Time more than 15 miles ahead of me and I knew this would be the last sighting until Mauritius. What lay ahead was a very daunting 3,400 mile sail on the notorious Indian Ocean.

Thursday 25th May 2017 Day 2
Run 96 miles
07:30 hours S 09 20 E 113 58
wind SE 5-10 sea1 metre sunny and rain squalls
heading 250 magnetic at 2 knots

The wind has remained light all day and in the

afternoon it dropped further requiring me to start the engine, which I ran until 21:00 hours. Having this obligation to John means that I now have to push Grace a little harder than normal as I do not want him to be waiting unduly for me, although he was quite adamant that I should not worry about this at all. His modern, large 16 metre yacht would make at least 20 miles more in a day than Grace would and also would be able to carry more sail area far longer in bad weather.

Friday morning, from 03:00 hours brought fresher winds and by daybreak Grace was moving briskly along at 6 knots in perfect sunny weather over a very blue sea.

Noon records a run of 117 miles and I log that we are enjoying a delightful sail with the wind just behind the beam on full main, stays and small genoa. This wind remained with us through Friday night and on Saturday at noon I write in the log that Grace has achieved an all-time record of 135 miles, noon to noon.

However, during the afternoon I had to replace the Aries paddle coupling and this required me to drift the boat for 2 hours whilst I removed the old and refitted the new one by hanging precariously over the stern, reaching down to the water level and having a spanner in each hand, leaving no spare hands to hold on with. The cardinal crime would be to drop one of these spanners into the sea! After this was done Aries steered a much straighter course, without the weaving from side to side that had been the case since Bali.

Sunday 28th May 2017 Day 5

Run 118 miles

07:30 hours S 11 25 E 108 13

2,970 miles to Mauritius

wind S E 20-30 knots sea very rough heading 260

magnetic

Squalls returned at 03:00 hours, so I had to put in a reef to the main, reduce the staysail and roll away the genoa.

I was delighted with our noon run of 118 miles, which is remarkable considering the drifting yesterday afternoon whilst I worked on Aries.

At 16:00 hours the wind has moderated to less than 25 knots and Aries is steering the boat so well that I comment in the log that this performance by Aries is as good or better than its previous best, as Grace drives ahead, reaching speeds of 7 knots.

On reflection, having been at sea for 6 days now, I believe that my decision to sail via the Cape of Good Hope was well taken, South Africa is a very beautiful country which I love and it will also be fantastic for Beebee because she will be allowed to leave the boat without restrictions.

Monday morning brought in a more overcast day with occasional sun mixed with rain showers. We are now 2,842 miles from Mauritius and Cocas Keeling Islands are just 442 miles away, which would have been a stop-over but because of my commitment to John, I will bypass these islands as well as Christmas Island. Nevertheless, I have decided to change course to pass close to Cocos in case of emergency.

Our noon run is very good at 133 miles and we have now sailed 599miles away from Bali.

On Friday the 2nd of June, is our tenth day at sea. We have 2376 miles to go and we have been averaging 115 miles a day for this period, which is very good, all be it most of the times have been very boisterous sailing in 5 metre plus swells.

These days are hard sailing but we are covering great mileages and I keep myself happy by looking forward to the return to South Africa, revisiting St Helena and re-refreshing my painting in the Azores. All sailors who visit the Azores are expected to paint some graffiti on the dock walls or the docks, representing their sail to these islands. I have refreshed my painting twice since it was originally painted by Marilyn in 2003.

This time I can add "Around The World" to it, putting it in the minority of the thousands of paintings, which have been painted over the years.

As always this hard sailing is taking it out on Aries and at sunset the coupling on the Aries paddle broke again and now I have no more spares having previously used the four spares that I carried. I worked until midnight making one by laminating epoxy resin and glass fibre cloth around an aluminium tube of the correct diameter. So, we are drifting again whilst I do the work. I kept Grace hove-to the rest of the night and at dawn on Saturday the wind picked up to 30 knots with strong squalls and heavy rain. At

BEYOND THE SUNSET

17:00 hours I hung over the stern and perilously fitted the new coupling in three to four metre seas, wearing a harness, as all of my upper body was outside the boat, taking all my strength to push myself back on board the many times it took to refit the coupling.

Regrettably, it broke immediately I attempted to re-set Aries, leaving me no choice but to try and make a stronger one. Fortunately, I carried good stocks of resin and cloth which to every sailor is a vital cargo.

Sunday brought with it improving weather and sunshine, so I was able to re-fit the coupling in the moderating swells, feeling very confident that this coupling would not break again. The previous 48 hours has been difficult in terms of the wind and rough seas which has meant remaining hove-to. I estimate that we drifted over 65 miles in this period, such a bonus, as it was in the right direction.

I wrote in the log at 16:00 hours that it was "wonderful to be underway again, sailing away from these aggressive seas instead of lying there, being knocked about by these waves."

Tuesday 6th June 2017 Day 14
Run 117 miles
08:30 hours S 15 27 E 93 18
Mauritius 2,066 miles
wind S SE 15-20 knots some breaking seas partly cloudy

We are two weeks at sea now and the Indian

3,400 MILES TO MAURITIUS

Ocean is living up to its reputation of big seas and
consistently strong trade winds. The evenings are now
much cooler in this 15 degrees parallel, Beebee is quite
happy to sleep in the cabin and because of this weather
she spends a lot more of her time below. This of course is
the southern winter and so I expect it to get colder as we
move south.

Grace's noon run of 118 miles is very pleasing and
I report in the log that at times Grace is surfing down
these big seas at ten knots. Last night was particularly
hard sailing, with waves throwing the boat off course
frequently, so I had to keep Grace on a dead run because
even when on a broad reach, once knocked off track, she
would be quite unable to recover, resulting in a mad
uncontrolled dash to windward, with all the sheets and
sails flogging in the wind! Not only is this deafening, wet
and violent but also very destructive for the sails! I
recorded in the log that these incessant wind and wave
days are very tiring and a few days of wind less than 15
knots, would be very welcome.

In a message on my tracker from Marilyn, she tells
me that John on 3/4 Time has sends his best wishes and
has my position plotted on his charts.

It is pleasing to have less than 2,000 miles to
Mauritius.

The next week brought little change in the sea
state or weather and we continued to experience rough
seas and strong winds, rarely having full sails up, instead
being double reefed most of the time. Wear and tear is

taking its toll on the boat's performance and we have developed quite a few more leaks from the decks than we previously had.

Our daily runs average near 120 miles, in spite of periods of having to heave-to in strong near gale force squalls. Aries ability is now becoming depressingly more inefficient requiring constant resetting and I know it is because of the sailing conditions, which have remained unchanged for the previous three weeks, causing huge wear.

I am now realising that these are Indian Ocean conditions, to make mileage one has to accept that this is how it is and I just have to get used to it! These big five metre steep swells are the norm here in this vast open ocean between India and Africa.

Friday 16th June 2017 Day 24
Run 94 miles
09:00 hours S 19 54 E 75 06
Mauritius 995 miles
wind 15-20 squally seas big

Whilst running with the staysail on the pole, a particularly vicious squall arrived without warning and severely damaged the sail, leaving it almost beyond repair, but in my book, as long as one has enough glue and repair fabric, nothing is irreparable.

The list of broken or damaged equipment grows by the day and my list of work to be done in Mauritius becomes longer and longer. I often need to remind myself of Just So, my first boat, the most basic of boats but we sailed her thousands of miles across oceans with no experience, no money and little or no equipment.

John had said that he would be in Mauritius in 25 days, so he should arrive there the day after tomorrow, with some luck.

Today I made a pledge to myself to get Beebee, and Grace back to Kefalonia, whatever it may take.

At 18:00 hours I write in the log – "*unbelievable, a cloudless sky, wind 10 to 15 knots, one metre swell, a lovely, sunny, warm afternoon!*" this gives me the opportunity to take down the staysail from the aluminium roller and get it into the cabin for repairs. We are sailing now on just one reef and half of the genoa. Today we are less than 1,000 miles from Mauritius, so it is all downhill from now onwards!

The following four days were so unlike the previous three weeks as we were now beset with light winds and calm periods and our daily runs were now under 90 miles or less, in spite of using the engine regularly. Furthermore, our water reserves were low and I had to seriously anticipate catching rainwater if the wind did not improve.

BEYOND THE SUNSET

Thursday 22nd June 2017 Day 14
Run 106 miles
09:00 hours S 20 38 E 065 45
Mauritius 455 miles
wind SE 15-201 metre swell clear and sunny

This fresher wind today is most welcome and our noon run is 106 miles, the first hundred in six days.

At noon I record that a large swell has come up from the south, so somewhere down there it is blowing quite strongly.

A message from Marilyn told me that John on 3/4 Time had arrived in Mauritius on the 17th of June, so he has already been there five days. My earliest anticipated arrival would not be before five days, unless we get absolutely perfect winds and we are not befelled by any problems during the next 467 miles to Mauritius.

The following three days were an answer to my prayers with the re-appearance of the fresh trade winds and we made good runs of 110 to 120 miles each day. On Sunday the 25th of June I wrote in the log: *"This afternoon and particularly this evening I am filled with a great feeling of joy in our achievement in arriving tomorrow in Port Louis in Mauritius, after 33 days at sea!"* This feeling of excitement and happiness is overwhelming, I suppose it is because we have knocked off a huge chunk of our circumnavigation. Durban is only 1,500 miles away, which is from where I left on Tumbler in 1983, so technically once there, I will have completed a circumnavigation, but not on Grace and not solo.

At noon, on our 34th day at sea I brought Grace alongside the customs dock in Port Louis, and was met by John Bouma from 3/4 Time. We quickly tied up Grace and when I stepped ashore, John handed me a large glass of cold beer, my first in 34 days!

BEYOND THE SUNSET

21

Mauritius and the return to South Africa

Port Louis is a very clean modern city and the area we are in was laid out more for pleasure boats, and the large ships were in a different part of the harbour. The waterfront area where we were was very much a tourist area, with an abundance of modern shops, restaurants and supermarkets.

John and I sat outside the bar about three metres from Grace and waited for the immigration officer, who has been summoned and was on his way, so we took this opportunity to enjoy a second beer.

A short while later, after having been checked by the immigration officer, I moved Grace into the marina, quite close to where John's boat was berthed. The following morning I completed my inbound clearance in town and then spent time with John who showed me where the banks, supermarkets and hardware shops were located.

During the next two weeks I was able to do most of the repair and maintenance work that was required on Grace, as well as sail repairs and mechanical work to Aries. John and I managed to see some of the island and spent many an evening together as well as a few days trawling the industrial area looking for boat hardware. He had a problem with his hydraulic auto pilot, so had to have engineers aboard his boat to remove repair and re-fit it.

Beebee was not allowed ashore but I disregarded this ruling and walked her daily within the immediate harbour area and she soon became popular with the other visiting yachts in particular with Georgio on a yacht called Fortuna, who obviously missed his own dog from home. We were fortunate to meet up with Georgio again in Richards Bay.

Port Louis is an amazing vibrant city, clean and prosperous, a popular tourist attraction for visitors from all over the world. The island of Mauritius is mountainous, tropical and well forested with good agricultural production. It also benefited from its close proximity to South Africa and I saw many South African products on the shelves in the supermarkets. There was a great variety of food available and John and I particularly enjoyed the spicy local dishes which were inexpensive in the fast food restaurants.

The inevitable arrived and on the morning of the 15th July, I said my farewells to John and other friends, also of course made my last skype call to Marilyn. John was intending to stay on in Mauritius a further 30 days, which was fine as I wanted to fly home to Greece from South Africa to spend time with Marilyn and also see my family in the UK.

What lay ahead was 1,520 miles to Richards Bay, by way of the bottom of Madagascar, a strong trade wind route and is known by reputation to be a hard, rough passage. All of the southern Indian Ocean is unobstructed by any land masses so the wave swells build over a fetch of thousands of miles. As well as this, three major ocean currents meet at the bottom of Madagascar, the South Equatorial, the Madagascar, and the Mozambique current which is the strongest of the three, running at times in excess of three knots.

We left at 15:00 hours from the marina, sailing on a beam reach in the lea of the island in a 15 knots wind, making an easy five knots.

I set Grace on a heading to a weigh point about 10 miles south of Reunion Island and from there we would swing on to a heading for the bottom of Madagascar, followed by a more westerly heading to Richards Bay, a total of 1,520 miles.

At noon the next day we were 29 miles from Reunion Island, the wind having remained a steady 15 to 20 knots since leaving Mauritius. At 13:00 hours we had already covered 104 miles, a good start at over 100 miles in 24 hours.

The following day, Monday, our first full day at sea has been a very good start to this trip, with a very kind wind, comfortable seas under sunny skies. All last night we enjoyed a beautiful broad reach sail on a steady 10 to 15 knot wind. A late moon gave us a bright sea and Grace was in her element making miles without fuss. Aries too, was working well, having benefited from a good going over in port.

I write in the log that *"I have no desire to shorten this circumnavigation and in the main, it has been most enjoyable, I do love sailing Grace and the more I do so makes me realise that this boat is much more capable than I realise and at times I let her down, so I must do better!"*

Tuesday 18th July 2017 Day 4

Run 70 miles

08:00 hours S 22 43 E 054 25

wind SW 5-10 knots sea flat trade wind cloud

Last night we were becalmed, drifting most of the night on a very flat moonlit sea.

This morning has brought a light breeze and we are sailing at 3 to 4 knots. The AIS is showing a surprising amount of shipping within 30 miles of us, so I need to keep a reasonable watch.

Grace is of course made of wood and these days wooden boats are very much in the minority, usually about one in thirty, and most sailors that I talk to think that I must be crazy to own one. But it has often been said, that to build an oceangoing wooden yacht is one of life's great joys, as wood is the most beautiful of mediums to work with. To sail such a craft, built by oneself is another joy, and to have these skills, time and good health to do a circumnavigation, is surely a great privilege and I consider that I am very fortunate to enjoy this and I count my blessings.

That evening I record in the log that I have had to run the engine all day as the wind remained very light. Surprisingly the night became quite cool and I continued to see a steady parade of ships, at times two at once would be visible within five miles of our position.

On the Wednesday morning, our fifth day at sea, I note in the log that I let Grace drift overnight in the non-existent winds, but was obliged to keep a constant look out because of the steady passing of ships. Our noon run of 87 miles is really very good as we had drifted for at least five hours.

Marilyn relayed a message from John, "*Light winds until Tuesday then strong winds from astern followed by tail wind 10 to 15 to Richards Bay*".

Saturday 22nd July 2017 Day 8
Run 30 miles
08:00 hours S 24 26 E 050 27

The last four days we have been plagued by light winds and an opposing one knot counter current. I have had to run the engine daily and during the last 2 days the counter current has been pushing against us incessantly at one and half knots so our mileage has been very disappointing

At 18:00 hours we seemed to have finally lost this opposing current and we are now making better speed, but what is unsettling is the arrival of large 1 to 2 metre swells from the south, which signifies stronger winds south of us and I remark in the log that the direction is not encouraging.

Our diesel tanks are now empty and I have resorted to pouring in 25 litres from my precious 100 litre reserve, which I keep in Jerry cans.

Sunday morning brings a clear sky and a slight sea we are managing to sail at 3 knots on a very light wind and the good news, is that we are definitely out of the opposing current which robbed us of our progress. Our noon run is 27 miles which is our best in 3 days, furthermore a southern current the Madagascar is back, giving us a slight push at half to one knot and I am hoping soon to pick up the south Equatorial current, which should also be beneficial.

At noon we are now 106 miles from our Madagascar way point, still suffering from the ever presence of a constant flow of shipping. The wind remained steady all afternoon and we enjoyed the surprising visit of a large whale just before dark at about 300 yards away, he remained briefly on the surface and then submerged, not to be seen again.

One of sailings great pleasures in good weather is reading without interruption, to digest, to think and live in one's memories.

Monday 24ᵗʰ July 2017 Day 10

Run 84 miles

08:30 S 24 51 E 048 04

This morning brings a very overcast sky and a south east 10 knots wind accompanied by a moderate swell. During the early hours a strong wind forced me on deck to change our full sail plan down to double reef which I had to keep in until dawn.

The distant profile of the high mountains of Madagascar became visible, barely distinguishable from the clouds, during mid-morning on the starboard bow more that 40 miles away. My intention is to maintain a distance of 30 miles from land but to avoid the extensive shoal south of Cape Santa Marie, though in fine weather I would have been happy to sail over it, as it is 10 metres deep, but bearing in mind that Marilyn's weather forecast strong winds for tomorrow, my preference was for deeper water.

Late in the afternoon I realised that we were picking up a strong 2 knots current which is pushing us due south taking me from my intended course and giving me little gain on our heading of 260 magnetic.

Sadly I have finished the last of Patrick O'Brien's books which have given me so much pleasure these last months. I have read his 20 volumes 3 times during the last 8 years, always reading his books whilst at sea.

Tuesday, our eleventh day at sea brought with it the strong winds, as messaged to me by Marilyn. The sea has become quite rough, at mid-morning I realised that we have lost the current as we are no longer drifting south, so we are now managing to hold the desired south westerly course. At noon I record that the wind in now blowing at 20 to 25 knots requiring Grace to be double reefed. We are making a speed of 5 knots on a heading of 260 magnetic.

During mid-afternoon I made the decision to turn south to avoid the Letoile Shoal. Even though pushing south will make it difficult to claw back our position against the Mozambique current to Richards Bay, but being caught in 10 metres of water, over a 50 miles area will be dangerous in breaking seas. We are about 40 miles from the shoal and having given it a lot of thought, I have decided to make the decision to turn south.

At 15:00 hours the wind was blowing strongly at 30 knots so I set Grace to heave-to, on a tack which because of the current now running at 2 knots should drive us south, avoiding the shoal.

Shortly before dark I was able to reset the sails, treble reefed and recommenced sailing as I felt we would now clear the shoal comfortably. Grace quickly picked up speed, making 8 knots in the current whilst I kept a close watch on our plotted position.

My AIS radar sounded an alarm at 22:00 hours, informing me that a ship was approaching on my stern. She was a large bulk carrier called Christina and my AIS radar gave me her speed as 9 knots, compared to our 8 knots. Less than one mile away, in this very rough weather, I decided to call her on the VHF radio and ask her what was her intention, as she would shortly run me down.

After some delay the officer on the bridge instructed me to hold my heading as he would swing behind me and overtake us on my starboard side. Immediately this struck me that this was an extremely dangerous manoeuvre as he was barely making enough speed to overtake or avoid me. When Christina was 0.6 miles away, on my stern I called him again and his response was, he would now swing to port and overtake me on my port side. The Collision Rules of the Sea state that "*an overtaking vessel must at all times avoid and not endanger the vessel that is being overtaken.*" I was fearful that if I changed my direction, this incompetent officer on Christina would make the wrong decision and run me down, so I told him once again that I would not alter my heading.

At this time another ship appeared 2 miles in front of me heading towards me and Christina and I realised this was one of the reasons for Christina's indecisiveness. Now, she at last became aware that she could not overtake me unless she increased her speed considerably and as I watched the AIS read out it showed me her accelerating very quickly from 9 knots to 15 knots giving her the speed to safely clear Grace on our port side passing a mere 250 metres away in very rough seas.

The wind from midnight continued to strengthen and I was forced once again to turn Grace on to a more southerly course. By 04:00 hours we were experiencing very big seas, some of which were breaking into a vast flurry of churning foam and so I decided to once again put Grace back into the heave-to mode.

Whilst hove-to, drifting at the mercy of the big seas on our bow brings home to me the reality of what circumnavigating is all about. It is easy to talk about it but the doing is somewhat different. In this situation I have to make an effort to remember that Grace is a well-built boat and I must trust in her original builder, who put his own integrity into the building of this fine boat.

Thursday 27th July 2017 Day 13

Run 30 miles

17:30 hours S 27 46 E 044 43

Richards Bay 669 miles

wind 25-30 SE sea very rough sailing 3 reefs

We remained hove-to all night as I considered the weather too strong for Aries to maintain the steering.

I spent the morning re-tensioning the rudder cable which has stretched badly and also replacing the steering ropes to Aries. This has resulted in an improvement and Aries is once again steering the boat on 280 magnetic. That evening the wind once again picked up to 30 knots forcing me to set Grace to heave-to. I do feel guilty about keeping Beebee down below in the cabin as it is far too violent on deck to take chances with her. Strangely enough she is quite accepting of this and shows no bother about not being able to go to the toilet.

Friday morning brought a reprieve in the weather, the wind dropping to 10 to 15 knots and the swell moderating to 2 metres.

We are now too far south of our intended track to Richards Bay which is 649 miles away, being on the same latitude, so we will have to sail well north of west, to counter the strong Mozambique current. I have set Grace on a heading of 300 magnetic but I still think that it is doubtful that we can push against this current, so probably we will end up south, having to go into Durban instead.

Noon brought a clearing sky and moderating seas, Aries steering well in these improving conditions and at 17:00 hours I record in the log that we are finally enjoying a pleasant sail in a SE 10 to 15 knot wind, with a much easier sea state.

Saturday 29th July 2017 Day 15
Run 111 miles
08:30 hours S 28 47 E 042 22
Richards Bay 538 miles
wind E SE 15-20 sea rough sunny double reefed

My noon run was 111 miles, a good one, but unfortunately we were unable to hold our heading, so we have increased our south position by a further 33 miles. The previous night was difficult, with less sleep, more jibes and ongoing steering problems. Aries is coping but not with its usual skill. The current is a steady 1.5 knots, pushing us south and compounding our problems.

I have realised now that I must jibe Grace on to the other tack to regain our north latitude as we are over 100 miles south of our original intended track to Richards Bay. At sunset I became aware that we were once again current free and I am hoping that this might last all the way to the South African coast, where I know that the current always runs strongly south. On conclusion I believe we have lost the Madagascar current but not yet found the Mozambique current.

Swinging on to the other tack has given us a heading of 330 magnetic, a speed of 5.5 knots and at 19:30 hours we are 502 miles from Richards Bay.

On Sunday morning we find ourselves almost becalmed so I have set Grace with the engine running on a heading 30 miles north of Richards Bay, to allow for the anticipated strong Mozambique current. Our noon run is a humble 63 miles but I have regained a fair amount of northing.

At 16:30 hours a cold wind began to blow from the SW at 15 knots which was a perfect wind to get us to Richards Bay. The current returned at 18:00 hours, so I decided to start the engine to give us additional push and at 21:00 hours I recorded, a surprising boat speed of over 6 knots on a heading of 290 magnetic, regaining a big chunk of northing.

Tuesday 1st August 2017 Day 18
Run 90 miles
09:00 hours S 27 46 E 037 40
Richards Bay 299
wind 10/15 E partly cloudy sea moderate

Last night was cold and damp and I struggled to keep warm but this was OK as we managed to do 109 miles since 09:30 yesterday, a very good run, as a lot of it was against the current. Aries is proving very difficult to set and is struggling to hold our course, which brings me to the conclusion that there is something definitely wrong with it.

At noon we are 288 miles from Richards Bay and we are in an unexpected strong current which is giving us a favourable push, so that our ground speed is 6 knots instead of 4 knots which it would be normally be in these circumstances.

Amazingly, in the late afternoon I recorded a run of 8 miles in one hour, so we are really getting a strong push from the current which must be running at a speed of 3 knots or more! Shortly after this I turned Grace to a 280 magnetic which allowed 15 degrees for current drift.

Wednesday morning brings us 195 miles from Richards Bay and we are blessed with a perfect east north east 15 knot wind. Our noon run is 108 miles which leaves 180 miles to Richards Bay so I am quite happy with our progress in spite of Aries barely working but somehow Grace is holding her course.

I am really excited with this coming landfall, as it brings out very profound feelings in me. This country of South Africa was my home for most of my youth up until 16 years of age, at which time my mother took the family back to Rhodesia. I returned as a married adult with our daughter and lived here in South Africa for 7 more years. I do love this country passionately for its diversity of people and unbelievable natural beauty, from magnificent mountains to stunning coast lines.

My concern now, is how long will this weather window last as it is common knowledge that the gale frequency on this coast is greater than 20 percent, especially at this time of year.

On Thursday morning, our 20th day at sea, we are motoring in calm and sunny weather on a flat sea. We lost the wind 2 hours before dawn and we are now 100 miles from our Richards Bay way point.

Aries is barely steering the boat so I have coupled Ray, the electric auto pilot in combination with Aries, in an attempt to hold our course. I am now confident that I can do this last 100 miles quickly because we will be turning soon and heading down current.

I feel overjoyed and exuberant to be returning to South Africa, in particular in the same way as I left it, on board my own sailing yacht.

In the evening twilight, a large whale appeared a few metres in front of Grace's bow, its huge back glistening and shining in the last rays of the setting sun. Then quite alarmingly it choose to surface with in 10 metres alongside the cockpit and I must confess that its proximity was frightening.

A 12 knots north wind had begun to blow at this time which is the best I could have hoped for and Grace is pressing on eagerly, making good speed down current.

At 05:00 hours on Friday morning 4th August, we entered Richards Bay in the dark shortly before dawn and proceeded to the small craft basin. In the first rays of sunlight as dawn was breaking, I arrived at the foreign arrivals dock and tied Grace up in a flat calm and very quiet atmosphere. There was no one about and the whole area was very still and peaceful. I was very happy to be here and enormously relieved to have concluded this difficult passage from Madagascar.

We had done over 90 miles from noon yesterday, a very good run helped by the strong currents.

22

South Africa

Our stay on the wall in the small craft harbour was to say the least, most enjoyable. The area was fronted by a large complex of restaurants and bars and behind these were beautiful large, mowed fields, with groupings of pine and casuarina trees. This area covered hundreds of acres and was boarded on both sides by lagoons. Beebee and I enjoyed twice daily walks over this vast area and we soon made friends with locals and other visiting yacht crews, enjoying the wonderful social life amongst the yachting community. Every Sunday, a group of motorcyclists would arrive at one of the bars, for a day of karaoke singing, filling the marina with the sound of pop classics perfectly sung. It was very enjoyable to sit on the deck of the boat with friends, listening to the music whilst drinking a cold beer in the glorious South African sunshine, creating wonderful happy memories. Beebee had free run of the marina area and soon became well known and quite spoilt by friends.

I returned to Greece at this time for a month via England where I spent time with my siblings Audrey and Doug, my children and grandchildren and Fiona, normally resident in the Virgin Islands, was in the UK at the time and so I was fortunately able to see her as well. My time with Marilyn and friends in Kefalonia went all too quickly and it was not long before I was back in Tuzi Gazi marina, waiting for John's arrival on 3/4 Time, to help him on his sail to Cape Town. During my time away, Beebee had been staying with Ian Morrow and his family, in Pietermaritzburg. Ian is my ex-wife's nephew, and I will always be grateful for the excellent care and love that Beebee received whilst I was away.

Regrettably John had severe rigging problems near Madagascar, and was delayed a further two weeks whilst getting temporary repairs done.

His arrival in Richards Bay was a happy day and we soon renewed our friendship, spending many evenings on each other's boats, or in the restaurants. His rigging was once again worked on and some of the shrouds were replaced. Whilst this was taking place and waiting for spares to arrive for his boat we decided to travel to the Drakensberg mountains, a beautiful area which South Africa is famous for.

I organised the rental of a car and a cottage on a lake near a town called Underberg, for the weekend. I explained to John that I had to visit a school in Underberg where I had been a border when I was eleven years old at a very sad time in my life. This, I said was not unlike a pilgrimage and for me would be a return to my past.

23

1952 Rhodesia

Doug, Audrey, Conny and Me

My earliest of memories, when I was six years old, are of driving in the early evening, almost dark, in the pouring rain. In the car were my father and mother, my older brother Doug, myself, my sister Audrey and my youngest sister, Conny. The road we were travelling on was hardly a road, but a track that my father had cut through the bush, to get to the mine. It was rough and at times under water and we frequently had to stop for my father to dig the car out of the mud.

Nobody was in a good mood and we children knew that it was very wise not to complain, as this would incur the wrath of both parents. The area we were travelling in was the tribal area known as Belingwe and was the tribal home to a scattering of rural farming Africans, living a simple life on this huge underpopulated reserve. The mine we were heading to, was known as the Malcolm Mine, named at the time of my birth and was on the banks of the Ingesi River, about ten miles from an American mission station, who were the only other white people on this side of the river. Beyond the Ingesi River was a town called Shabani, about thirty miles away, where my two sisters were born, at the time when my father worked on the Shabani Asbestos Mine.

We eventually arrived, very tired and hungry at our new home which consisted of two mud and lath rondavels (round rooms) separated by a rectangular room, which was the living room and the rondavels were the bedrooms.

The roof was made of locally cut thatch grass and it was for this reason that the kitchen, a small similarly built room was located ten metres away, standing on its own. The only other structure was the toilet, known as the "long drop", was a one metre square room also constructed of mud and thatch, which boasted a wooden seat perched over a deep pit and was located ten metres away from the house. We, of course had no running water and all water for bathing and cooking had to be hand carried, brought up from the river.

On arriving at our new home, my earliest memory of a home, my siblings and I were quickly put to bed after a simple meal prepared by the "cook boy" a man in his sixties from the local tribe. All the lighting was done with candle or paraffin lamps and once these were extinguished only the stars would shine down on our humble home, far from all civilisation.

My father had been prospecting and running the asbestos mine for a few years before deciding to move the family there. He had originally discovered an outcropping of serpentine, the asbestos rock from which the fibre is extracted whilst prospecting the area for gold. Now he had in place a rock crusher, powered by a crude oil engine and a system of separating the woolly fibre by blowing the crushed rock, mostly dust through fine metal screens which captured most of the fibres. These would then be scraped off the screens, bagged and sold as unrefined asbestos. The market at this time was strong for the product and so my father had set up the mine, plant and house to be our way of life for the foreseeable future.

My mother had been born in Australia and spent most of her life in Scotland on the Isle of Skye where she did her schooling; my mother's family were Mc Crimmons, which was an old Skye family known for the piping school which taught the bag pipes. She had met my father, a Rhodesian air force pilot, in London during the war. Now he was ten years older than her and at the time of their marriage in London, during the second half of the war, she was only nineteen years old. When the war was over, she moved with my father to Rhodesia, to set up married life and raise a family in quite primitive conditions on the family gold mine near Fort Victoria. My brother and I were born in quick succession, being only twelve months apart.

Apparently the gold mine did not do so well, so the family moved to Shabani where my father found employment on the Shabani mine, an asbestos mine, and here my two sisters were born.

Life on the Malcolm mine soon developed a routine, with home school for my brother and I and long days playing in the surrounding wilderness for the four of us when my mother's patience had totally worn out. She was the first to admit that she did not have the patience to teach. Once a week my father would take the 5 ton truck to Belingwe, our nearest town, twenty five miles away, to buy supplies.

This town had a small population of about thirty families, a single hotel, a petrol station and a general store. A police station kept law and order, most of the problems were caused by drunken white farmers or miners. There was a magistrate's office, visited on occasion by a travelling magistrate, and of course there was the District Commissioner who with his staff and messengers kept some degree of law and order amongst the rural tribal people. The occasional violence would take place amongst the tribesman and this would be resolved by the D. C. and the magistrate.

The police station consisted of three or four white

police officers and about eight or so black constables who would patrol the reserve on their bicycles.

The weekly visit to Belingwe was done to resupply from the general store for the family as well as to buy food rations for the black mine workers who my father recruited from the reserve. They lived near the mine in rondavels very similar to our own home, in a small community on the river. They numbered about fifteen families, most with children, living a very primitive life, growing their own food and keeping livestock for milk and meat. The trip into Belingwe would always result in my father getting drunk and my long suffering mother trying to talk him into leaving the bar before closing time. Also, on the back of the truck would be five or six mineworkers who would catch a ride into town to buy items for the community at the mine. These were the first signs of the beginning of my father's deep alcoholism, that eventually would cause so much suffering to the family, which my mother always thought had started during the war. In today's time it might be diagnosed as war stress or P.T.S.S. as my father had been shot down in his bomber over Abyssinia, badly wounded and spent days in the desert before getting back to his lines. I believe the gunner had been killed at the time.

Life at the mine was very hard for my mother with no other white people within ten miles with whom she could socialise. However, she would meet regularly with the African women, who would come to the house to trade for basic items like sugar, salt and dress cloth which my mother bought in bulk. For this she would receive in trade fish from the river and grown foods from their fields, including "gaka" a type of sweet cucumber, ground nuts, black and brown beans which we called "niamors" and sweet corn as well as other grown food. The odd old rooster or fowl would also arrive for trade.

My memories of those days are of happy times with my brother and sisters, also of family times on Sundays, when we would go down to the river to fish for bream under the large shady trees which covered the high banks of the river. The deep pools in the wide Ingesi river was also home to a group of hippos, so one would have to be alert to this threat because these animals can be very dangerous at times. I do remember my mother telling of the time when they had to drop the fishing rods and run, to get to away from a charging bull.

My brother and I would often accompany my father down to the mine, so I became familiar with the routines at the mill and in the quarry, which was in the riverbed, where the serpentine rock was blasted free by my father, to await crushing. He also employed women to hand pick the long surface fibre from the rock before crushing, who were paid by the bag, for their days work.

There was also quartz rock out-croppings within a few miles of the mine, which can at times be gold bearing, so in the evenings my father would often return home with a bag of rock, about the size of a 5 kilos flour bag. He would crush the rock with an iron pestle and mortar and then proceed to pan it, looking for gold traces. Doug and I would watch this procedure in keen anticipation because we knew if gold was found it would offer a second mining operation and would lead to great benefits for the family, but always my father would pour out the residue from the prospectors pan and mumble something which we knew was a no. We both found this quite disappointing, I suppose that, to six and seven year olds, life is very simplistic.

Unfortunately, our uncomplicated life was to end in tragedy and would change everything.

It was a Saturday afternoon and my father was in Belingwe with the truck getting the usual supplies from the general store. My mother and the four of us children remained on the mine and it was shortly after lunch whilst we were resting in our bedroom, my mother in hers, during the afternoon heat. We became aware of my mother at the front door and she called out to Doug, in a thinly disguised alarm: "*Fetch Dads gun and the magazine, quickly now*". It had also become known to me and my siblings that an African tribesman was a few yards from the front door.

How long he had been there, or how long my mother had been aware of his presence-I do not know. Furthermore, I was not aware of there having been any previous conversation with this man. We all sensed, as children do, the extreme urgency in the situation and we were all quite fearful. Audrey was five years old but knew of what was going on where as Conny just sensed some imminent peril. I knew as well as Doug about the gun, a Beretta 9 millimetre pistol, as in our small house with its lack of furniture, there were no secrets. Once my mother had the loaded gun we were told to go into her bedroom, close the door and stay there.

To this day I do not know exactly what followed or what had already happened as this was never discussed. We children only ever discussed what had happened that hot day on the Ingezi River, when we became adults and never in the presence of my mother. My father, prior to his death never ever discussed it either.

My next clear memories were of my mother telling Doug to go to the mine and summon Samson, who was the "boss boy" (foreman). Doug ran the half mile to the mine compound where the workers lived and shortly Doug returned with Samson who was told to ride his bike to the Mission at Menene and summon help. No explanation was needed as to the urgency of the situation, as the mine workers, seeing Doug on his own knew that something was seriously amiss. We children were told to remain in the house and not to go outside under any circumstances. A while later the people from the Mission arrived, two men and a woman, and if I recall correctly about an hour later two white policemen arrived with two black constables, accompanied by my father.

There was a lot of serious talking and I believe that the African man's body was placed in the back of the police vehicle. Statements were taken from my mother and father and shortly later everyone left and the family were now on their own.

I have a clear memory the following day of our cook boy boiling a blanket in a cut down 44 gallon drum on a wood fire behind the house, the water was very red in colour and there was a strange sweet smell in the steam. Two mine workers were spreading blue gravel which was the residue from the crushing process at the mine, over a large area of the yard, which was quite obviously soaked in blood.

It was less than six months later that we were all once again loaded into the car and followed the truck on which were the family's possessions, up the track leaving the mine and the reserve forever.

My mother had appeared in the Magistrates court and was acquitted of manslaughter. It was deemed self-defence, notwithstanding that the dead man was known to be mentally unstable. This was gleaned from overheard conversations by other adults in Belingwe and our future home in Que Que.

My father had taken up employment with his brother, my Uncle Charles who owned and ran a quarry supplying road stone to the Government in the Que Que region. Mother had secured a job in an office in the town and the family now lived in a prefabricated house built by Italian prisoners of war. These were called Pisa Houses, maybe they had a slight tilt like their namesake in Italy. Doug and I were in school and Audrey and Conny were looked after by an African maid whilst my mother was at work.

It was maybe a year later that new plans were in the air regarding our family. Rhodesia at this time was going through an economic slump, as was a lot of the world in the early fifties, but Australia was offering free passages to immigrant families to help fill and develop that large continent.

We as children, were now told that the family were going to live in Australia, this marvellous country across the sea, where it was as sunny as Rhodesia and where Dad could get a good job. At times he would joke and say things like "*even on a hot day you would still need to wear a jumper to keep warm*" which lead me to think that my father was not that enthusiastic about this move. He after all had been born in Africa of Scottish parents and only knew Rhodesia, except for the war period when he was flying bombers for the Royal Air Force.

In due course we all boarded the train in Que Que, which over two days, took us to Johannesburg in South Africa, following a change of trains and a further two days, we arrived in Cape Town. From there, an hour's ride on a coastal railway brought us to Simons Town, where we moved into a holiday camp, known as Gay's camp, consisting of wooden bungalows set amongst tall pines not far from the beach.

This whole experience of riding in trains, living within a hundred yards of the beach with this vast panorama of dark blue water was amazing and exciting to us children. There never seemed to be a dull moment in our lives at this time.

So, now the family stayed in Gay's camp for a couple months, waiting for our tickets to go on a passenger ship to Australia.

On the main road above the camp there was a

fruit shop and the wonderful smell of grapes, pears, plums and other delicious fruit which all grew in the Cape was a huge attraction for me and my siblings. As a treat, my mother would buy us fruit quite often, these luxuries had never been available in such abundance in our time on the mine. Simons Town had a large fishing fleet which fished in these rich cold Cape waters so we often had fresh fish on our table which my mother bought from the fish monger located alongside the fruit shop.

My father with time on his hands seemed to drink heavily and was away from the family most days. I think he was trying to obtain work, because there was a huge row with my mother when the paperwork, which qualified him as an electrician, could not be found amongst our packings and suitcases.

My siblings and I spent many days on the beach with my mother, meeting people and playing with other children so life was one long holiday and one of our great interests was collecting the multi-coloured seashells. Simons Town was and still is, a quaint historical seaside village, set in a beautiful part of South Africa.

It eventually became clear that we were no longer going to go to Australia and to this day I have never found out why this did not happen. Nevertheless, we were once again on the train with all our belongings, heading off to Durban in Natal Provence. My Dad had a sister in Durban as well as many cousins and I think this was the main reason for leaving the Cape.

We stayed with my Aunt Tubby on arrival in

Durban, after a month my parents bought a house in Fig Tree Place in Umbilo, a southern suburb of Durban.

We now had a permanent home which was within walking distance or a junior school and my father secured a good job complete with a van. The area we lived in boarded on the very extensive industrial district associated with Durban Harbour, the largest in all of Africa. Doug, Audrey, Conny and I were soon in enrolled in a junior school and so our lives became routine and normal, definitely in comparison to the last few years.

What should have been a settled time in our lives did not become so, primarily due to my father's ever-increasing drinking and a slide into total alcoholism, which had a very destructive effect on the family.

He had no control over his drinking whatsoever and in spite of him being very skilled at his work and a very intelligent man, his days of drinking binges would eventually cause him to lose his job.

The firms he worked for gave him repeated opportunities to keep his job, forgiving his irresponsibilities many times, but always he would drift back into oblivion. Repeated visits to sanatoriums to dry out and admission to hospitals to heal his alcohol damaged organs failed to change him from this path to destruction.

The effect on the family was to drive us down into total poverty, because all the money which came into the house from his and my mother's earnings would be drunk by my father in the form of cheap South African brandy.

It was not long before other people noticed how unkept and scruffily dressed my siblings and I were at school. We always wore the oldest school uniforms and owned just one pair of shoes each. We as children did not make friends easily and never brought friends home from school. This resulted in the four us becoming very close and bonded siblings, shy of outsiders and other families. We have always remained close.

Family deprivation from alcoholism is not an uncommon story so I will not go further into details of our home life but only to say that my father's abuse of my mother would eventually cause her to take my brother, sisters and I to stay with the family of an "Alcoholics Anonymous" member, who took us in.

Following this my mother decided to send Doug and I to government boarding schools which were free of charge (in our case anyway).

The school clothing list which was given to my mother to ensure we arrived with the correct clothing items, was way beyond her financial means so that the family we were staying with and other AA families, made sure Doug and I arrived at the boarding schools with all the required clothing items, neatly labelled with our names. It was never understood by Doug and I why we were sent to separate schools, over a hundred miles apart and the school I went to was a day's ride in the bus from home. Because of this Doug and I would only see the family and each other during school holidays.

The school that I was sent to in Underberg

accommodated about 50 mixed sex boarders in separate buildings, the boys in a modern two storey building and the girls in an older single storey building, where the two matrons also lived and where the sick rooms were located.

All the boarders were bussed from Durban to the school and by the time I arrived on the bus, I was filled with profound home sickness, the reality of no longer being with my siblings dawned on me and this always affected me throughout my time at Underberg.

The school was located in the foothills of the beautiful Drakensberg Mountains, a dairy farming area near the tiny village of Underberg, it being the community centre for the district's farmers. The grounds were very large, I would guess at about a hundred acres, half a mile outside the village, over-looked by a small mountain. On the other side of the school the land dropped away steeply down a ravine to the river, a half mile away. The whole area was captivatingly beautiful and the school grounds were boarded on all sides by mature firs and pine trees, some over 25 metres tall.

Discipline at the school was strict, I found this out on my first day by talking in the communal showers and was immediately caned by the supervising matron on my wet bare behind. How was I to know that talking was forbidden, as I had only just arrived hours before? In spite of harsh discipline, the food was good, the dormitories were comfortable even though they were unheated in winter, the snow often lying 30 or 40 centimetres on the ground.

The classrooms held about twenty pupils and two years were taught in one classroom. The teaching staff numbered three teachers plus a headmaster, who would on occasion fill in for an absent teacher.

On Sundays we were given free rein but climbing the school mountain "Hlogomo", or walking down the ravine to the river were always compulsory, shepherded in turn by a teacher. All the teachers lived in the school in small apartments which were attached to the dormitories.

I cannot say that I enjoyed my time at the school, but I did love the wilderness and panoramic beauty which surrounded us. At the end of term, we boarded the bus and were taken back to Durban for the school holidays. I was delighted to be reunited with my mother and siblings but I did not see my father during this time as he was hospitalised in a sanatorium.

The second school holiday at home my father was again in hospital and it was planned for the family to visit him on the weekend, but a visit by the police during the week informed my mother that he had passed away. Our family, I believe felt a great sense of relief, but Doug my older brother had been always been favoured by my father and I knew that he took his death very hard.

When I next returned from Underberg it was to a rented house further out of town, as my mother had sold the Figtree Place house. I never did see again the family who had so kindly taken us in during those bad days.

Our lives began to improve and my mother was able to secure a well-paid job which lead quite rapidly to her promotion to manager. The firm was an agency for a sewing machine company, small but very busy.

Doug and I finished our school year at our boarding schools and were enrolled in a local school. Dare I say, once again a routine settled in our lives and my mother continued to do well in her job.

It was during my second year at high school that my mother and her new partner, Dieter, a German man younger than her, decided that the family would return to Rhodesia, to live in Salisbury the capital. The family nostalgically always considered that Rhodesia was best, so a return to our home country in spite of having to change schools again was decided by all as a good move.

Dieter married my mother and was good to her for the remainder of her life. Doug, Audrey, Conny and I finished our schooling, went to college and married in Rhodesia.

24

Memory lane in the Drakensburg Mountains

John and I left Richards Bay early in the morning on Friday, driving to Petermaritzburg, then on to Underberg in a rented car. We had Beebee with us on the back seat and I was really looking forward to the weekend ahead of us. On approaching Underberg town, I was amazed at the beauty all around us and ten miles in front, the panorama of the Drakensberg snow-capped mountains was breath taking. We drove to the school where I had been a pupil as a nine year old, at the time of my father's death. John and I had some difficulty in finding our way to the school buildings as the immediate area was now quite built up with houses and the roads had also been realigned. We were met by the headmaster at the security gate after ringing the bell and on explaining that I had been a pupil here over sixty years ago and would love to take a trip down memory lane and walk around the school, his response was very welcoming.

John stayed for few minutes talking to this very kind gentleman, whilst Beebee and I quietly walked across the playing fields where I once played all those years ago. The buildings were unchanged, still the old red brick style favoured by the government at the time but new additions were now obvious. I was overwhelmed by memories, long since buried in the past and at times felt once again to be the nine year old home sick boy separated from his family. On re-joining John and the headmaster, he explained that the school was now much smaller and used only for day pupils, the dormitories were long since unoccupied.

We walked through them, now empty rooms, as was the dining hall and the prep room. Proceeding then across the old football field to the three original classrooms which now had the addition of two new ones plus a new office block.

The basic essence of the school had not changed at all and it was easy to be transported back in time to a period sixty years ago, which brought back memories of my childhood at home, my father and the hardships my mother had suffered, leading up to becoming a pupil at this school. John also felt the nostalgia of the moment and seemed also to enjoy this visit in this lovely part of the world.

We thanked the very kind headmaster and left the school for the last time, proceeding into town to buy our provisions for the weekend.

We found our cottage on the lake, about fifteen kilometres from Underberg, located in the hills on an unspoilt lake and river scene and beyond this, a few miles in the distance, were the magnificent Drakensberg mountains. The cottage was thatch roofed spacious and well fitted out with all requirements. The only other person to be found was the caretaker who made up the fire in the central wood-burner, which kept the cottage comfortably warm. We strolled amongst the pines and the willow trees down to the lake and drank in the surrounding beauty. Beebee was in her element and we had her running to and fro chasing sticks thrown by us and also the bird life which was in abundance.

The end of the day was spent watching the sun set over the lake from the front lawn of our cottage, whilst drinking a few beers and keeping an eye on our steaks cooking on the charcoal grill. A perfect evening, without doubt, one of the best I experienced on this circumnavigation.

Enjoying a few beers with my friend John Bouma

The rest of the weekend was spent hiking over the magnificent mountains with Beebee and exploring the area, enjoying the breath-taking views in clear warm days.

Monday saw us driving back to Richards Bay and we immediately began the preparation to leave on John's boat, 3/4 Time for Cape town. John had the rigging work done which was required, but the rigger said that on arrival in Cape Town, it was imperative that all the mast rigging must be replaced by the specialist company, which was located in Cape town. John was quite happy to do this because what lay ahead was a daunting long sail back to North America.

The day of our departure arrived and I moved on to 3/4 Time. We cast off the lines from the wall at Tuzi Gazi, proceeding to motor out into the channel. Beebee was once again staying with family and I would retrieve her in about 10 days when I returned to Richards Bay to pick up Grace and start my own sail for the Cape.

Disaster struck immediately, no sooner had we cleared the channel and put up the sails when an explosive bang sounded quickly followed by a large section of the main mast rigging cables dropping on to the deck!

We frantically took down the sails to get all the weight off the 22 metre mast, which was bending and flexing, threatening to collapse on us at any moment, as it had now lost much of its support. After rigging temporary support to the mast John turned the boat and we slowly motored back to the wall. It was very apparent that the boat now required completely new re-rigging, which had to be made up and sent from Cape Town, taking at least another month.

I could not wait any longer, as my South African Visa was about to expire, so John kindly released me from my obligation to sail with him to Cape Town. I collected Beebee from Ian Morrow who had so kindly cared for her on these occasions and straight away I made my preparations to leave for the Cape while the weather was still good.

Three days later on the 7th December 2017 I bade a sad farewell to John and many other friends made in Richards Bay and Beebee and I left to continue the circumnavigation. My intention was to closely watch the weather, stopping in the ports of East London, Port Elizabeth and Mussel Bay before rounding Cape Agulhas and proceeding back into the Atlantic Ocean.

25

The South African coast

Once we had cleared the channel and I was back at sea I was looking forward to the challenge of this difficult coastline but still feeling sad about leaving Richards Bay which had been one of the best times on this circumnavigation.

The weather forecast was not the best as the weather window was only two days before it would deteriorate, hopefully we should get to East London in time. From the onset the wind exceeded 20 knots and by the following night was blowing at over 30 knots, forcing me to heave-to. On Saturday morning I was able to hoist sails again, all be it treble reefed in rough seas. At noon we experienced a wind shift to south west and by sunset we were once again hove-to, our second gale in two days. At midnight I released Grace from our hove-to status and we continued sailing in heavy seas and high winds. We experienced breaking seas and continuous strong winds, the boat down below was wet and uncomfortable from water getting in through the leaking hatches and elsewhere.

Noon the following day, Sunday 10th December

found us close hauled against the south west wind in very rough and breaking seas. Typical of bad weather on this coast is that, it is short lived and by noon the wind and sea had moderated considerably.

Monday morning brought with it very light winds so we were barely making two knots. I was unable to start the engine and I suspected that I had a failure in the forward pair of batteries which seemed to be flat. This problem caused me to sail past East London as I was unable to fight the strong current. My next option was Port Elizabeth.

A message from John warned me of impending extreme weather, strongly advising me to get into Port Elizabeth by dawn on Wednesday. John was aware of my position because he followed me on my satellite tracker.

Tuesday 12th December was a sunny day, fortunately as the batteries were very low, quiet incapable of starting the engine so I hoped the solar panels would put enough charge back into the batteries to get the engine started. The wind was from the west at ten knots but the current was against us so were are only making three knots and I needed to get into Port Elizabeth in good time, or if not I anticipated heading off of the coast into deep water, rather than be caught on this coast line in bad weather. I decided not to attempt to start the engine but rather wait until sunset to get maximum solar energy into the batteries first. This I did and after a short prayer at the very last crank the engine fired up to my great relief! I decided not to hang about and motored at six knots towards Port Elizabeth as the forecasted strong gale was only hours away.

At 02:00 hours on Wednesday morning I tied up Grace at the Algoa Bay yacht club having motored nonstop. There was no one to help me because of the early hour but fortunately there was absolutely no wind. I immediately took to my bunk so happy to have made it into this secure marina in front of the gale.

We stayed four days, waiting for good weather and also topping up our diesel and water tanks. I decided to push the boat out by buying a new battery, which I would only ever use to start the engine, hopefully of avoiding a repetition of the anxious previous days. I was shown great kindness by the members of the yacht club who were willing to run me around in their cars to do my shopping.

I left at 11:00 hours Sunday 17th December and headed out on a misty grey day in a very light wind but we were soon making over six knots in the strong Agulhas current. The wind remained light and cold all day but picked up overnight giving us a steady six knots until dawn.

Monday remained cold and grey with no wind and poor viability forcing me to run the engine all day making a steady five knots in the favourable current. That evening at sunset we were sixty six miles from Mossel Bay.

Tuesday morning found us only six miles from the breakwater at Mossel Bay having made good mileage through the night. We tied up in the commercial harbour at 10:00 hours as there was no provision in the small yacht club harbour for visiting yachts.

My 7 day stay in Mossel Bay was most enjoyable. The town was clean, quite old fashioned and could not be described as bustling. Beebee and I enjoyed some good walks around the area and spent most days exploring. There were no other yachts in the harbour, so from that point of view the days leading up to Christmas were very quiet and I felt a little lonely, however I was invited to a very sumptuous Christmas lunch on board the neighbouring tugboat. The food was truly excellent, prepared by the full time cook who made sure we had a Christmas lunch to remember with his five courses. The crew were very friendly and I was touched by their kindness to invite me on board to share their feast, they had noticed that I was alone on this Christmas Day. The function of this tug was to service the offshore mooring buoys where the tankers would discharge their cargos.

Later that afternoon I walked over to the yacht club with Beebee and was able to wish Marilyn, my family and friends season's greetings via the internet.

After having my batteries checked, which were found to be in good order, so with little else left to be done I headed out on the 26th December bound for Simons Town. It was a sunny cloudless day and a light southerly wind was blowing on the beam which kept us moving at a pleasant five knots, a very enjoyable sail.

At sunset I recorded in the log that we were now 97 miles from Cape Agulhas, the most southern point of Africa, which also has a reputation for being one of the most stormy capes in the world. This is Africa's Cape Horn, always a challenge for yachtsman and fishermen.

On Wednesday 27th December noon found us still 23 miles from Cape Agulhas, the wind remaining very light all night barely giving us steerage. Shortly before sunset Cape Agulhas was visible on the starboard beam and I now turned Grace back into the Atlantic Ocean leaving the Indian Ocean behind us.

The following morning we were off Cape Hangklip, which is the entrance to False Bay, 22 miles from Simons Town, our destination. The overnight sail was very pleasant even though I had to always keep a weary look out for shipping as this area around the bottom of Africa is usually very busy. I expected to be in the Simons town marina, known as False Bay yacht club by noon but an hour before the wind freshened rapidly to near gale force making it dangerous to attempt an entry into the marina. I decided to phone the yacht club, as friends of mine, Bob and Patricia Harrison had previously made arrangements for a berth at the marina. These friends, Marilyn and I had known in Florida in 2002, so I was really looking forward to meeting up with them again. The yacht club said they would send a tender and crew out to bring Grace into the marina and I was assured by them that the competent crew did this on a frequent basis in this windy part of the world. The tender duly arrived and with great expertise brought Grace into the berth in a 30 knots wind which I was informed was a very regular occurrence here.

The following morning Bob arrived at the club and

we enjoyed a wonderful reunion over lunch. In the afternoon Patricia joined us and I spent a very memorable evening with them at their lovely home which overlooked False Bay.

On Saturday night I was invited to the home of another pair of friends who Marilyn and I had met in St Martin where they had lived before returning to Simons Town.

Their names were Gary and Muriel and they had also been sailors having originally sailed from South Africa to St Martin. It was great fun catching up on the years which had intervened since St Martin days and I will not forget a very memorable evening.

Beebee and I did a lot of walking in the Simons Town area and I tried to find the location where my parents and my siblings had lived after leaving Rhodesia in the early 50s. The holiday camp was no longer there but shops and roads in the main were unchanged, bringing back memories again from my childhood over 60 years ago. I was invited to spend New Year's Eve with Bob and Patricia, and after dinner we all proceeded to a friend's home joining a group where we celebrated the arrival of the New Year. The party was very lively and I felt so fortunate to be amongst this group on such a special occasion.

26

Cape of Good Hope to St Helena

On Friday 5th January 2018 Beebee and I left Simons Town after saying goodbye to Bob and Patricia on the dock at the marina. The wind was SW at 5 to 10 knots so we were close hauled all the way from False Bay to the Cape of Good Hope, about 12 miles away. We picked up a favourable current which turns around the bottom of Africa and I also had to be sure of avoiding the rocks about 2 miles off the Cape. These submerged rocks Doug and I had almost collided with in Just So forty years ago.

I set our course for St Helena and felt sad at seeing the South African coastline fading into the distance at sunset. I have a great love for this country and I must return again to enjoy its beauty, to me the most beautiful of all countries.

On Saturday 6th January I recorded in the log that we drifted from midnight until this morning due to no wind. We still had no wind and we find ourselves in a miserable cold drizzly rain so I have set Grace to run on the engine at idle speed. Once again I found the forward battery bank seems to have no charge but I know that the batteries are in good condition as are the solar panels, so there must be a problem in the wiring but I am still unable to locate it.

Shipping was frequently visible, always one or two to be seen, as they bottle neck around the bottom of Africa.

Sunday brought drizzle rain once again with little or no wind all day until late afternoon when a westerly wind of 10 knots gave us a boat speed of 5 knots on our heading.

Tuesday 9th January 2018 Day 5
Run 103 miles
09:00 hours S 31 20 E 014 59
wind S 30 knots sea rough
treble reefed heading 300
speed 5.5 knots

Aries has coped well, steering on a dead run in the strong wind.

All around us is a heaving, occasional breaking iron grey sea under a low stormy sky. Grace is driving forward with very reduced sail area, surprisingly managing to hold course in these very hostile conditions.

By early evening we were experiencing a full blown gale and at this time waves were continuously knocking Grace of course, far beyond the ability of Aries to recover. So I set Grace to heave-to for the night. We remained hove-to overnight, enduring the occasional breaking wave on deck, but Grace as always coped well in these violent conditions.

Wednesday brought with it a great improvement in the weather so I re-set the boat to sail on 3 reefs and with a further dropping of the wind at noon I was able to shake out a reef. Later in the afternoon the wind dropped to a pleasant 15 knots and with it came a much more settled sea so we were able to enjoy far less stressful sail under clear skies with lots of sun.

Monday 15th January 2018 Day 11
Run 126 miles
09:00 hours S 22 48 E 08 50
wind 15/20 SE sea moderate sunny little cloud

The wind for the last 5 days has remained fresh at 20/25 knots most of the time giving us good runs and at times very pleasant sailing. Our run for the last 3 days was 391 miles which is averaging 130 miles a day, I think a 3 days record for Grace.

This is the same track that I sailed on Just So with my ex-wife Penny, my daughter Fiona, who was then just 4 years old, and Conny my younger sister, now passed away, who was accompanied by her boyfriend Brian. Tragically he was killed 3 years later in a helicopter accident in Australia.

Just So was a primitive boat, having a tiny 9 horse-power engine, a single battery and no electronic equipment whatsoever, not even a communication radio. But she was a strong boat, very seaworthy and in her we sailed many thousands of ocean miles, spending time in the West Indies, the Bahamas and eventually arriving in Florida where we sold her for what it had cost to build. Once Just So was sold we returned to South Africa, Durban, where my son Neil was born six months later. Our lives were now a far cry from those carefree vagabond days of living in the islands on Just So, changing to an urban existence, living in a house and setting up a new business was a different challenge.

The following 4 days gave us good mileage with good runs and strong winds, fortunately nothing over 25 knots. I am back in ocean passage mode and once again enjoying life on the high seas with the return of confidence which is quickly lost after a long spell onshore, particularly amongst older sailors. We are back to routines of sail changing, navigating, boat repairs, cooking and of course reading books whenever possible. I no longer keep a deliberate watch at night, because for the last week we have not seen any marine traffic as we are now out of the shipping lanes.

On the 16th January, our 12th day at sea I realised that I had incorrectly entered the co-ordinates of St Helena in the navigation GPS, substituting the W prefix for E prefix, that is the West for East and my repeated checking of the numbers failed to spot the error! This would have been picked up on a daily plot on paper charts but over confidence on my part is what has led to this blunder. I did not have a paper chart but this is no excuse as I could easily have made a plotting sheet. This mistake has added at least 4 days to this run!

Beebee requires no encouragement to sleep below decks, most likely because of the cold nights. She snoozes all day in the cockpit and I do try and give her a lot of attention, I feel guilt that she cannot run about as she is normally a very active dog. Nevertheless, she does seem quite happy and content, because after all, she has my companionship all the time.

Thursday 25th January 2018 Day 21
Run 118 miles
St Helena 62 miles
07:30 hours S 16 21 W 04 48

The previous 10 days sailing has been very pleasant in these warmer trade wind latitudes, each day much the same as the one before with a steady SE trade wind blowing, under sunny skies. Grace has maintained good mileage runs each day and life on board has been uneventful and relaxing, with my days spent locked in the fantasy world of books. I have enjoyed these days of perfect sailing which this part of the Southern Atlantic Ocean is renowned for. This morning we are now only 62 miles from St Helena and I see an opportunity to possibly make the St Georges anchorage by night fall. I can only achieve this by running the engine at medium speed.

St Helena is a very high mountainous island and on a clear day can be seen from 40 miles away. I detected the distinct profile of the island amongst the clouds late in the morning.

I remember the joy and excitement at my first arrival here, our first land fall on Just So with Conny, Brian, Penny and Fiona. In those days all navigation was done on paper charts using a sextant and site reduction tables, not without embarrassment, I must confess I did a better job of it then than I have done this time, with the use of modern satellite technology.

Conny and Brian continued with us on Just So to Brazil, where they left the boat to explore Brazil and travel by other means. Just so was only 10.02 metres, about 32 feet long so it was cramped living for 4 adults and a child. Unfortunately, 2 months later Brian and Conny separated. Conny went to the UK to work in an office and Brian returned to Australia to learn to fly helicopters.

Conny passed away in 1999 suffering from Cancer and it is for this reason that I use this sail to raise money for Cancer Research UK. Grace was Conny's middle name, so her spirit now lives in this faithful little boat. She was to have attended the naming ceremony but sadly died 3 months before Grace was launched in the UK.

Conny my younger sister

This pending arrival on Grace does bring back many memories, there is nothing like the first landfall in a sailing boat after a long ocean crossing and doing it on Just So was really such a proud moment for all of us that day. However, I did return once again to St Helena on Tumbler my second boat with Penny, Fiona and my son Neil on our way to America from South Africa.

Just before sunset I picked up the mooring in the anchorage with the help of James who owns the business called "St Helena Yacht Services". James had seen my approach when I was still a mile away and motored out in his dinghy to meet me, instructing me to follow him, taking me to an available mooring. He is also a keen yachtsman and I had the good fortune to meet him in Richards Bay while he was doing his own circumnavigation with his wife and children. He is from St Helena, having been born on the island.

St Helena

Over the next 5 days I enjoyed walking and exploring the island which had largely remained unchanged from my first visit nearly 40 years ago and I struggled to identify any new buildings. This in my opinion was a good thing, because the charm of this island, is its unspoilt heritage and its historic buildings from Napoleon's time when he was imprisoned here by the British at the end of the Napoleonic wars. His home at Longwood is maintained in its original condition by the French government. The island has its own charm and it is definitely a British out post cut off from the world, preserving its uncomplicated way of life which is reflected in the kindness and friendliness of the inhabitants. St Helena is now of course connected to the world by the new international airport so one must expect changes in the future.

27

Atlantic sailing to the Azores

Thursday 1st February 2018 Day 2
Run 100 miles
09:00 hours S 14 36 W 06 52
heading 303 T
wind light SE 10/12 2 m swell rainy

We left St Helena yesterday morning in a light SE wind. Our water tanks were filled up and so were our food lockers in anticipation of a non-stop sail of over 45 days to the Azores. I did not take on my full quota of diesel as fuel was expensive here so were the groceries, St Helena having to have all its goods shipped from South Africa as little food seems to be grown on the island. Charges for moorings, in my opinion were high, at £10 per day, considering we must also buy compulsory medical insurance and pay for the ferry connection to the moorings, as well as charges to clear in and out. I am sure that these charges encourage visiting yachtsman to keep their stay quite short, which sadly does not benefit the small local businesses and restaurants.

We are now into a long sail, the longest I will ever

do in my lifetime, taking over 6 weeks and a lot of it will be against the wind. The route direct to the Azores is rarely done by yachtsmen because most yachts prefer the downwind route via the Caribbean and Bermuda to the Azores, longer but with good winds and many stopping off places.

It does require a mind set and some mental fortification. I have in my Kindle many books by popular authors like John Grisham so I anticipate a lot of reading will be done in the weeks ahead!

The sails and sheets (ropes) are very worn, particularly the staysail which is now at the end of its life and I know that equipment problems will be my biggest concern over the coming weeks. Diesel tanks are not full but an extra 100 litres over this distance will have little effect.

I had set a way point near Cape Verde about 1,085 miles from St Helena, so in an emergency I would be passing close enough to divert to the islands.

On Saturday, our 4th day at sea I recorded in the log that I am having battery problems again, the forward battery pair seemed to be not charged up for some reason. Without decent batteries Grace's bilge pumps will not run and she does after all require frequent pumping to stay afloat. The rest of the day was spent changing the solar panel regulator and checking the wiring but still the fault eluded me. I was very aware that the environment we were in was hostile and a few equipment failures in succession would quickly lead to disaster. There was no help at hand

and I had to rely solely on myself and the equipment and spares that I carried on board.

The following morning I eventually found the problem, which had been plaguing me since Richards Bay. It all came down simply to a bad earth connection on the engine. This was easily and quickly rectified giving me the use of our forward batteries which turned out to be in excellent condition.

Tuesday 6th February 2018 Day 7

Run 99 miles

08:00 hours S 07 39 W 11 54

wind SE 12-15 knots sea 1 metre heading 310 T

We maintained a good course, running with the gib on the pole, Aries coping well through the night in the steady winds. Our position is on the same parallel as Ascension Island, which is 150 miles west of us. This tack keeps us east of my original intended track but that is ok, as it will give me the space to bare away west if the wind becomes, as it will eventually, more from the east.

BEYOND THE SUNSET

28

1982 Ascension Islands

Being so close to Ascension Island does bring back memories of the time I made landfall there on my previous boat Tumbler with Penny, Fiona and Neil, in the year of 1982. We arrived there despite advice at St Helena that yachts were not welcome at Ascension because of the military situation from the recently concluded Falklands war. For this reason we were the only yacht in the anchorage but there were a few military ships anchored in deeper water including one Maersk Ascension, a semi-permanent moored tanker containing military aviation fuel in case of a flare-up in the Falklands. The British crew on board were bored and lonely from the months at anchor and so the captain was very happy to have us on board for dinner and sent out a large launch to collect us to take us to the tanker, anchored 2 miles offshore.

We were thoroughly spoilt with luxury food not found in our larder! The children were delighted with the quantity and variety of ice cream available on the menu.

The only challenge, was that after being picked up by the tankers launch we had to climb the pilot ladder stretching 10 metres up the sides of this huge tanker. The children and I tackled this ladder with glee, Penny needed some coaxing but the anticipation of good company and a change in diet definitely helped her make the climb. Our return to Tumbler was made much easier as the captain had arranged for us to board the launch on the tanker's deck, which was then craned, complete with crew and passengers down to the water, thus avoiding tackling the pilot ladder in the dark after more than one gin and tonic! We did reciprocate by having the first officer and the captain on board Tumbler for drinks and dinner. This particular evening the anchorage was teeming with military security vessels, due to the presence of a member of the British royal family, Prince Andrew, who had flown to the island to join the convoy travelling to the Falkland Islands to re-join his helicopter squadron. We were advised on the radio by the military authorities not to leave our boat whilst Prince Andrew was proceeding through the anchorage. I suggested to Hugh, the captain of the tanker, that I would like to convey a message to Prince Andrew wishing him bon-voyage and to this Hugh said protocol would not allow it. But when the launch with Andrew on board passed within 10 metres of Tumbler Hugh lost self-control (maybe due to half a bottle of sherry) leaped to his feet yelling out loudly "*Good evening Sir*" to which a faint reply was heard "*Good evening.*"

The following morning we left Ascension Island taking with us fond memories of our short stay and some luxury items on board kindly given to us by Maersk Ascension.

During the next few months we sailed through Brazil, and then on to French Guiana where we anchored off the islands known as Ile du Salut, Ile du Diable, known as Devil's Island, made famous by the movie Papillon starring Dustin Hoffman and Steve McQueen. The film brought to attention the primitive penal establishment where long suffering French criminals were locked up in barbaric primitive stone cells far from civilisation. This prison was closed during the 1950s and the island is now uninhabited. The family and I explored the island over the next 3 days whilst anchored in the bay. The prison cells, solitary confinement cells and administration building occupied a large part of the island and were very extensive with inter-connecting paved roads and walkways. Most of the structures were now over-grown by the equatorial rain forest trying to reclaim the island. The whole place, to say the least was very eerie and creepy and one could sense the ghosts of the past, a place full of bad Kama. After leaving Devil's Island we proceeded through the West Indies and the Bahamas and spent many months island hopping before our arrival in Florida, America. After 2 years in Florida having sold the boat we moved on to North Carolina and set up a small business in the furniture industry.

In 1987 we left America and went to live in England to be near the family who had all moved from Rhodesia to England. Fiona and Neil carried on to eventually complete their schooling resulting in degrees from Cardiff university

29

The Equator

Friday 9th February 2018 Day 10
Run 100 miles
08:00 hours S 04 10 W 014 56
wind S 10-14 knots sea flat

Today we find ourselves sailing in very light
southerly winds on a flat sea. Our noon run is a satisfying
100 miles and I was able to refit the staysail which I had
taken down the day before to do repairs to it. Sadly, its
condition is very poor so I need to make sure that I roll it
away before the onset of strong winds. The day is hot, to
be expected as we are now 4 degrees south of the equator
and this area has a reputation for being windless,
nevertheless I will not start motoring until we are north of
the equator if I can help it.

Beebee is quite relaxed these days and seems
totally at home on the boat. She is happy, cheerful and
always affectionate, so I do spoil her by adding a little of
my dinner to hers at meal-times. She is brushed twice a
day, as she is a malting machine, she should be bald as a
billiard ball because of all the hair that she has shed,
which has been blocking up the cockpit drains.

As we approach the equator the weather has got
much warmer and I anticipate being in the Northern

hemisphere in about 4 days. There will be a likely hood of doldrums beginning soon and this squally windless situation could go up as far as the 7 degrees parallel.

The following morning I reset our heading to cross the equator more west than originally planned, having consulted "Ocean Passages For The World" a British Admiralty publication, which recommends that north bound sailing ships should cross the equator at 25 degrees west longitude.

Today I had a saltwater bath on the deck as the weather is definitely hot enough, fresh water for washing is strictly disallowed. A swim in the ocean would be wonderful but as I am single-handed I could not bear the thought of being parted from Grace and Beebee should something unfortunate happen, leaving them to fend for themselves.

I write in the log "*It is so amazing that Grace sails without any attention day and night steadily from sun up to sun down, always quietly gliding along and the miles run under the keel without fuss or bother.*" St Helena is now a distant memory as we left nearly 10 days ago, so in theory we could be almost a quarter of the way through this sail to the Azores but I am in no great hurry as I will never in my life have time to enjoy a sail like this again.

In the afternoon I hoisted a "fisherman" sail which was given to me by a middle-aged Scandinavian man who sailed with a friend on a big 45ft modern boat. I met them in Panama at Shelter Bay, they did not really mix with other yachties but often ate on their own in the yacht club, always bringing the leftovers for Beebee.

Our boats were both hauled out in the boat yard at the same time and the chatty one, I cannot remember his name, would often come over with a couple of tots of rum while I was working on Grace. He very kindly gave me a large quality steering compass which I nearly sold in South Africa but I am so pleased now that I did not. Such a kind generous, quietly spoken man with a great sense of humour. He had worked on Irish fishing trawlers for many years so had lot of stories to tell.

The "fisherman" sail I would set as a "genaker" and it worked well in that role but as it was large and made of nylon it was only good in very light winds. This type of sail is also known as a mizzen staysail, filling in the gap on a ketch between main and mizzen.

On our 13th day at sea I record in the log "*I need to continuously remind myself to enjoy this time on this placid ocean and these weeks of relaxed easy sailing, without the stress of shoreside living, doing what I like. I should not count days and hurry things along, but rather enjoy reading books and living this simple solitary life in all its perfection. It will soon be over and never again will I have the ability to do this, even now the days flash by and it seems no sooner have I entered a new date in the logbook than I am doing it again, almost without pause.*"

BEYOND THE SUNSET

Thursday 15ᵗʰ February 2018 Day 16

Run 36 miles

09:00 hours S 00 17 W 019 44

wind calm-E 5-10 sea flat overcast and rainy

The previous three days we have been beset by frequent rain squalls between calms with the result we have struggled to make miles, averaging only 30 miles per day and drifting in calms during the night. We will cross the equator later today and I should not complain about the lack of wind, as this equatorial area is known as the doldrums. In these conditions 30 or 40 miles per day is not that bad going as it has been known for boats to drift for days or even weeks without any wind at all.

The following morning we found ourselves 14 miles north of the equator having crossed it overnight. At noon we were drifting having lost the wind again so I decided to run the engine at idle speed to help us get out of this doldrum belt and also to charge the batteries as we have been without sun for the past 4 days. The day is overcast with occasional rain but at times a slight north east breeze picks up and then dies. Could this be the beginning of the north east trade winds which I expect to find about 200 miles north of the equator.

My slow progress, watched by family and friends on my tracker, has caused some concern about my food and water stocks. So I sent a text to Marilyn re-assuring her that things were fine and my food and water was adequate.

I record in the log on our 20th day *"I don't get up and down at night to set sails unless it is really worthwhile as this is often a fool's errand depriving me of sleep and most often does not create any mileage in this location."* We are at the mercy of every rain squall with its constantly changing light winds and flat calms, all in the space of 30 minutes.

It became apparent that after tacking against the north wind, close hauled, that we were making no miles against the wind even though the boat speed showed 2 knots. I concluded that we were caught in the Canary current or the equatorial current which was against us and this became obvious because the GPS heading and the compass disagreed by 30 degrees.

Thursday 20th February Day 21
Run 38 miles
wind N 8-10 slight swell clear and sunny

A much more promising morning than of late and Grace is making 3-5 knots motor sailing. The northerly wind has remained with us all day encouraging me to think that we may be nearing the end of the doldrums belt. (I.T.C.Z.)

On Wednesday morning the wind was still with us having stayed steady overnight which gave us a steerage bonus of 15 miles. Our noon run was a pleasing 55 miles but during the afternoon the rain squalls returned and we once again lost the wind through the night. Thursday morning promised a better day with clearing skies and a very light north east breeze.

A tiny, deep ocean bird, a little larger than a sparrow but with small webbed feet came on board during the night. I found it sitting in the corner of the cockpit with fluffed up feathers, quite oblivious to Beebee's and my presence. It appears to have a broken leg and most likely will be dead by tomorrow. It is quite possible that we may have run it down while it was sleeping on the water.

At noon all signs of rain had disappeared and we enjoyed a peaceful sunny afternoon motor sailing with the help of the 8-10 knot wind.

Friday morning was once again overcast with light rain and the wind blowing north west at 8-10 knots. Grace is close hauled on the port tack, making 2.5 knots on a course of 350 degrees true. Our daily run on our course heading was only 26 miles but the good news is that we gained 40 miles in a northerly direction since yesterday, despite our overnight glacial speed barely managing to maintain steerage.

At noon we find ourselves struggling in heavy rain and frequent squalls. I found that we could not make any speed on a westward tack due to the equatorial counter current, so I changed Grace to an easterly tack which allowed us to motor sail at a speed of 4 knots.

Our little guest (bird with broken leg), hobbled to the rail from its cockpit position and much to my amazement, took flight in a spectacular display of high speed darting and swerving, just like swallows catching airborne insects, vanishing high into the twilight sky, such a display of the joy of life.

Generally, I am enjoying the sail and Grace is proving reliable as always. My mind set, should be not to count the days or expect better performance but to take what there is and enjoy what we are doing.

I am starting to see a lot of Sargasso weed, most likely brought down from a north latitude by the counter current. Days go by now without any sightings of ships and surprisingly we have not seen any dolphins or other marine life.

Sunday 25th February 2018 Day 26
Run 49 miles
08:00 hours N 04 10 W 22 26
wind NE 5-10 sea 1 metre swell cloudy

For the previous 12 days we have made low mileage due to the Inter Tropical Convergence Zone (doldrums) but hopefully since we have crossed the 4 degrees north parallel we could now be leaving this area of calms behind us. I have done a check on our food stocks, as I confess, I have become a little worried about it being sufficient to take us to the Azores, still 2,600 miles away, which will take at least another month. Beebee might have to share my food as our dog food supply looks questionable, this of course would suit Beebee admirably as she is always convinced that my dinner is more tasty than hers.

At 15:00 hours we are enjoying a sunny afternoon and Grace is sailing on a beam reach at 249 degrees true making 3 knots on a steady north east 8-10 knot wind. The engine is off which makes this sail one of the most pleasant in a long while.

30

29 Days

On Monday I record that our noon run was 66 miles and the wind remains from the north.

A message from Marilyn, once again she is concerned about our slow progress and wants to know if I intend to stop at Cape Verde for supplies. I hope my reply was reassuring, saying that a stopover there was not really on the cards at this time. My big concern is that the wear and tear on Aries, is considerable and should it fail to continue working I would have a very serious problem.

That night I enjoyed a beautiful moonlight sail, very quiet and smooth with Aries holding a good course over a flat sea. Now that we are crossing the 6th degree parallel I anticipate the winds becoming stronger and as we approach 27 degrees west longitude which "Ocean Passages For The World" advise as the best longitude for north bound sailing vessels.

I realised that at 60 miles per day we will not get to Azores in under 40 days, so I need to try and increase our average speed before our food and water runs out.

On the 28th February our 29th day at sea the wind is east north east 8 to 10 knots and its mostly sunny.

I write in the logbook that I believe we could now be in the north east trade wind belt which is good for our destination, but nevertheless we need the winds to be stronger to compensate for the days when the wind will be very light. Also, we need to cross the Azores high pressure zone which lie between 20 degrees and 30 degrees north parallels, known as "The Horse Latitudes", notorious for light winds and calms.

I have on board 100 litres of diesel fuel in drums, specifically ring fenced for the Azores high pressure zone. The fuel tanks are just about empty. We are now 1,755 miles from St Helena and 1958 miles from Azores as the crow flies, but in reality 2,400 miles.

On Friday 2nd March our 31st day at sea since St Helena we enjoyed a run of 84 miles, our best in quite a long while due to the consistent north east wind, which has been steadily strengthening over the last 4 days giving us improving daily runs.

It is now required that I swing Grace to a more northerly heading, which brings us almost to close haul sailing, meaning that life on board will become much more uncomfortable. I could postpone this course change but then we run the risk of being too far west and also making it harder to get to Cape Verde should an emergency force a stopover there. We should now be in the equatorial current according to "Ocean Passages For The World".

A stopover in Cape Verde would be a nice break and I could re-stock, but it would put us far east and it would be difficult sailing north from there against the Canary current and prevailing winds. To there from here would mean a very hard sail directly into the wind, so all things considered it does not really look like a good option, unless in an emergency.

The wind today is lighter than the last two days giving us a reduced run of 60 miles.

Our food stocks should last until the Azores but water will be borderline, so I have resolved to try and catch rain water, though rain has been scarce for the last week or so.

On Monday, 5th March, our 34th day at sea, the water tanks ran out, so now we are down to our reserves in drums which totals 80 litres.

In the last 8 days we made over 500 miles which I am pleased with as most of the winds have been light and all our sailing has been to windward.

Today brings much fresher winds at 20 knots with a rough sea, making it an uncomfortable sail. I suspect that this will be normal in the coming weeks so we will have much harder windward sailing causing greater wear and tear on the equipment.

The next morning I record in the log that the previous 24 hours has been a hard windward bash at a steady 3.5 knots. This has paid off, giving us a good run of 91 miles, very pleasing because it has all been against the wind. Today at 10:30 hours we are 1,635 miles from the Azores.

Thursday 8th March 2018 Day 37

Run 73 miles

08:00 hours wind NE 10-12 knots heading 335 T

This trade wind is steady and reliable and has given us another good run of 73 miles.

I could really kick myself for not keeping the water tanks topped up in the rainy doldrums belt, but such is hind sight. It never occurred to me at that time that our present latitude is a desert and rain is not plentiful, so now I am rationing our water consumption and the big problem with this is that one cannot enjoy a cup of tea at liberty, but must always remain with in the daily allowance of 2.5 litres which has to be shared with Beebee and the cooking.

The following morning I attempted to turn Grace to an easterly heading for the Cape Verde Islands but found to my horror that the best the Canary current would allow was 130 degree true, at least 30 degrees south of the heading to Cape Verde, caused by the strong southerly current drift. This would result in me passing far south of the islands. I turned Grace back to our westerly tack of 330 degrees true and decided to wait and try again later in a few days after getting more northing in the bag. So every gained mile was hard fought for.

On Sunday our 40th day at sea I listed the options in the logbook which we have open to us.

1. Press on NNE against the strong Canary current and NE trades heading for Cape Verde Islands.

2. Press on NNW heading out of the Canary current hoping for better winds and then swinging on a heading for the Azores, or Madeira but Madeira is 2000 miles away, which will really stretch our water ration.

In hindsight, I should have made much more westing, which might have kept us out of the Canary current but according to "Ocean Passages For the World" this current is very broad and stretches a long way west.

I attempted to go on to the port tack again to see if we could make Cape Verde from here but once again the current pushed our heading south, so we would in all likelihood pass too far south of Cape Verde islands, missing them completely. Whilst Grace was headed on this tack I was able to retrieve 20 litres of water from the water tank, where previously, the pump could not reach. This was such a bonus so now our water reserves are again back to 30 days.

On Monday I decide that we would stay on our north west heading out into the Atlantic, hoping to lose the Canary current and find better winds and greater chance of rain. It has become apparent that Aries is not working well and in spite of checking lines and lubricating the equipment, I fail to achieve better performance from it. Its efficiency is down to 50% of normal and if we were sailing downwind Aries would definitely not be able to steer the boat. Furthermore, I had to take the staysail down for repairs 3 days ago and Grace is now sailing without it, which really effects our performance. I am waiting now for an almost calm light wind day so that I can refit it.

Wednesday 14th March Day 42
Run 56 miles
08:30 hours N 17 26 W 34 33
wind NE 10-15 sea moderate sunny

At 13:00 hours the wind moderated enough for me to refit the staysail, so we are now back to full rig and I have set Grace to a more windward heading of 320 true on a starboard tack making nearly 4 knots.

The consistency of these trade winds is quite amazing and in spite of being close hauled for days on end, the alternatives could be worse. Our heading to the Azores now looks a lot better in the new light of the increased water reserves but nevertheless we still may not have enough water for the whole trip, particularly as we soon will be coming into the notorious horse latitudes, the area well known as the desert of the seas. We have had no rain for 18 days so I have decided to delay the decision whether to head for the Azores, or turn west for Madeira or even east for Cape Verde. In two days' time when we cross our outward bound track from the Canary Islands I will then make my choice.

Thursday morning brought an overcast sky and a fresh north east trade wind blowing at 15-20 knots giving us nearly 5 knots on a heading of 340 degrees true. This is our best speed in weeks and I believe that we could possibly have lost the cursed Canary current. Our noon run is 80 miles, the first decent run in 2 weeks. I was starting to believe that Grace's windward performance is poor but no, I see that given a full sail plan and reasonable wind she is not that bad. This improves my confidence and will help in my choice whether to press on north rather than turning back to Cape Verde.

Friday 16th March 2018 Day 44

Run 88 miles

At 08:00 hours the wind is north east, blowing at times to 20 knots and we are steering 337 degrees true in rough seas, double reefed. We are frustrated by occasional light rain showers but in this wind the rain is vaporised leaving, nothing to catch.

At noon the wind eased to 10 to 15 knots and it was time to make the decision whether to turn south east to Cape Verde to re-stock with water and provisions or take a chance on the weather and keep going for Madeira or the Azores. Cape Verde is only 600 miles away but the downside is that when we leave we will be fighting the strong Canary current and very fresh head winds which always blow in this area.

Azores is 1,200 miles and to go on to the Azores I must average 60 miles per day in order to get there before the water runs out. This distance of 1200 miles is as the crow flies but in reality it will be more. Furthermore, I must allow for the Azores high pressure zone, where there is often no wind for a week or more, so a healthy safety factor in my water calculation must be put into this equation. Our remaining water on board is 85 litres which at 2.5 litres a day will give us 34 days. I expect the wind to change, that is, go on to the nose or become much weaker with extended calms. This area was known in sailing ship days as the "Horse Latitudes" because when wind and water were in short supply, the horses and livestock on board the ships would be thrown overboard, unthinkable in modern times.

I made the decision at noon to carry on to the Azores and disregard the other options as I believe that the 50% safety margin in my calculation will be enough.

Saturday 17th March 2018 Day 45
Run 65 miles
08:00 hours N 20 57 W 36 19
Azores 1,077 miles
wind 10-15 NE sea moderate sailing 320 T at 3 knots

At noon I recorded another 70 miles for our 24 hour run so we are getting closer to the Azores but now further from Cape Verde with each passing day. I am of course always optimistic that the wind will eventually swing behind the beam, or at least to the beam which would give us improved daily runs. It is surprising that the wind is still blowing north east in this position so far from the African coast.

The good news today is that Grace has circumnavigated the planet by crossing our outward bound track, done in March 2016.

On Wednesday 21st March our position is North 25 degrees 34, West 35 35 and we are now 851 miles from the Azores. The previous 4 days has given us a total run of 131 miles in the steady east north east wind which has allowed a far more direct course. The sea has remained rough and I record in the log that we have been sailing against the wind now, for over a month.

The decks of the boat are always wet and water has found its way below through leaking port holes and hatches, making my bunk and most of the boat damp with no chance of it drying out because of having to keep Grace all closed up against the invading sea. So this part of the sail has proved to be a challenge which has become wearisome. A break from this continuous pounding against the waves and wind, living at 20 degrees of heal would be most welcome, even if we are becalmed and running on the engine. We are 50 days at sea now, definitely the longest sail I have ever done, but I expect once we lose these easterlies and find ourselves in the horse latitudes, complaints will also follow!

I sent a message to Marilyn today "*very hard sailing strong head winds always but ok.*"

At 17:00 hours I write in the log that we have done in the last 7 days and average of 60 to 70 miles per day to windward in trying conditions, all in all not a bad performance considering we have been reefed most of the time as well!

Our remaining water totals 65 litres which is good but our food stocks are low and all luxuries are long gone, leaving only pasta, noodles, rice and a slim choice between canned vegetables, tinned sardines, pilchards and corn beef.

Monday 26th March 2018 Day 54

Run 50 miles

07:00 hours N 30 25 W 35 53

wind NE 8-10 sea calm sunny

We have at last crossed the 30th parallel so we should soon lose the north east trade winds. Our run is 50 miles and the reason that it is lower than the previous days, is due to the lack of the staysail which ripped 4 days ago. I have been unable to remove it from the aluminium furling profile because it has somehow become jammed in the track. This sail is sorely missed as it is worth 10 to 20 miles a day on its own. I started the engine this afternoon for the first time in a month and motored until 23:00 hours, then a breeze allowed us to sail with Aries self-steering at 1.5 knots until dawn.

On Thursday, our 57th day at sea the wind was very light north north east so I took the opportunity to climb the mast and release the staysail which had been jammed for 5 days. It was quickly repaired below decks, using fabric and glue and I reset it but not in the furling profile but rather loose and "flying". This was a great achievement and I am very happy to have the full rig at my disposal again.

Our run today was a humble 48 miles but only 30

in the direction of the Azores. I believe we are once again pushing against a half to one knot current.

Yesterday the engine over heated for the first time this trip, I discovered the coolant was low, so I had to top it up with one day's water ration. I have diesel to motor frugally through the Azores high pressure zone but I have decided not to waste it when there is any wind or against any currents, but rather use it only when I can get the best benefit out of it.

On Friday, day 57, we woke to a sunny day and unbelievably the wind had swung to north west, allowing me to set Grace for the first time on a broad reach, that is, with wind behind the beam. Even though the wind was only about 12 knots, by idling the engine as well we were making over 5 knots for the first time in 30 days. Unfortunately, Aries has great difficulty holding this course which I had thought previously might be the case. Grace will steer herself to windward quite well but not downwind without the assistance of Aries. The afternoon was spent tightening the rudder cables and the Aries lines.

The weather deteriorated in the evening and the wind swung back to north east so I was able to get Grace to steer herself again, all be it double reefed in squally weather and mounting grey seas. The weather continued to deteriorate so I was forced to set Grace to heave-to for the rest of the night.

At 09:00 hours on Saturday the wind had swung back to north west at 10 to 15 knots so I set Grace on to a beam reach, giving us a good heading and speed. I noted in the log that it was very cold overnight, confirming that we are in the northern hemisphere winter.

31

60 Days

Our water stocks are now down to 43 litres which should get us there barring any unforeseen problems. We are now 358 miles from Horta, on the island of Faial, part of the Azores.

Sunday 1st April 2018 Day 60
Run 57 miles
09:00 hours N 34 40 W 33 46
Azores 331 miles
wind NE 15-20 cold grey overcast sea rough big swells

The 57 miles noon run against the north east wind is good and pleasing, particularly as we were treble reefed in rough conditions overnight. The staysail halyard is jammed at the mast head, so to get it down I need almost calm weather, in the meantime despite my best efforts at wrapping the sail and halyard around the stay, parts of the sail continue to flap in the wind. Late in the afternoon the weather once again deteriorated, so much for the calms in the Azores!

On Monday I recorded another run of 56 miles leaving 275 miles to Horta. The wind overnight had dropped after 21:00 hours to almost calm so our run is once again good. I am convinced that these slow days are due in some measure to barnacle growth on the bottom of Grace because whenever I look over the side, I can see large areas of the hull covered in barnacles. In previous times I have found that any growth robs Grace of speed and furthermore it also makes it difficult for Aries to steer the boat. One thing that has also been proved to me that Grace will only perform well if she has a decent staysail.

It seems that the antifouling paint that was sold to me from a large drum from which the seller had de-cantered my 10 litres, was very poor quality. I had bought this paint from the boat yard in Richards Bay. It should have stopped barnacle growth on the bottom of the boat for at least a year, particularly as we had been always on the move. The lesson here is to never to buy antifouling paint from an open drum!

On Tuesday, our 61st day at sea we are becalmed in cold but sunny conditions on a big rolly sea running from the north west, so this means that there is wind somewhere in that direction. Our run today is a paltry 38 miles, mainly due to us drifting without wind from 22:00 hours through the night.

These very calm conditions allowed me to finally get the staysail down and begin the repairs. This effort required climbing the mast five times to unjam the sail from the aluminium foil, not easy in these rolly sea conditions! So now we have only the main and the yankee jib (small genoa) as our working sails. Unless we get a good tail wind our progress will only be around 50 miles per day giving a predicted arrival in 4 or 5 days, using our diesel very sparingly! At 22:00 hours I record in the log that the wind is blowing from the north west at 10 knots and we are broad reaching on a starboard tack at last.

Wednesday 4th April 2018 Day 62
Run 55 miles
12:00 hours N 36 17 W 31 16
Wind W-SW 15 knots sunny

Aries is struggling to steer the boat and I notice that it requires a lot of rudder to respond, which tells me that the bottom is covered in a large amount of marine growth.

The wind has continued to increase and by mid-afternoon we are forced to heave to as the wind is now nearing 30 knots. Our drift is 40 degrees magnetic which is in the right direction and at times reaches speeds in excess of 3 knots. By midnight the wind force has reached full gale strength bringing with it big breaking seas! This is not the weather I was expecting when we are only 150 miles from the Azores!

Thursday 5th April 2018
08:00 hours N 37 01 W 30 35
Azores 128 miles
wind NW gale force sea very rough hove to

Our drift is basically in the direction we want to go, so that is the one good thing in this bad situation. Our noon position puts us at 120 miles from the Azores but the wind has strengthened even more and the sea is even rougher with waves frequently breaking on the deck. I have no choice but to keep Grace hove to and trust in her integrity to keep us safe in this strong gale!

At 08:00 hours on Friday morning we are 85 miles from the Azores and thankfully the wind had dropped in the early hours of the morning, now down to 25 knots. I have managed to get Grace sailing again albeit in very rough sea conditions, still carrying a treble reefed sail plan. The sky is grey and very overcast and it is also bitterly cold.

Saturday 7th April 2018 Day 66

08:00 hours N 38 05 W 28 56

Horta 29 miles

wind W SW 10 knots motor sailing at 5 knots

The wind dropped to 10 to 15 knots overnight bringing with it much calmer seas making for a much easier night. At 08:00 hours, we are only 29 miles from Horta town on the island of Faial.

Pico, the high island which lies a few miles to the east of Fayal, became just visible poking above the clouds at 09:00 hours and shortly later I could make out Faial directly in front. I felt truly exited, but also quite relieved that this marathon sail was now coming to an end. Such a successful outcome to 65 days at sea, enduring more than half of it against the wind and currents.

Horta has rated in my book as one of the best
landfalls for a long distance sailor and on my three
previous visits always felt most welcome. The welcoming
marina staff and immigration officials have a lot to do with
this and the fact that this is also a true cruiser's marina,
as almost all the boats are from somewhere else. It offers a
very convenient mid-Atlantic stopover for the scores of
yachts crossing the North Atlantic each year. The charges
are inexpensive and the facilities are very good, with
wonderful hot showers and self-service laundry. There is a
bar and restaurant located in the very spacious marina
area, which is beautifully laid out with an abundance of
lawns and gardens. This bar is a favourite hangout for
yacht crews to swap their stories and make new friends.

Now, what this marina is really well known for, are
the hundreds of paintings done by visiting sailors, which
cover every pavement and wall throughout the marina,
producing a most colourful, amazing patchwork of art
which is so unique! I too have a painting which Marilyn
painted in 2003 which had been refreshed twice since, so I
am hoping that it has not been overpainted.

At 17:00 hours I tied up Grace to the customs
dock in Horta marina. I was tired but happy at the
completion of this long sail which has ended so
successfully.

Beebee and I stepped off Grace and after clearing
formalities we walked over the lawns towards the bar. It
was an unbelievable feeling to be back on land and I am
sure Beebee felt the same, judging by her cantering freely

about at high speed. She has of course been here before and I am quite sure that she has not forgotten her previous time here.

I felt so proud of my little boat, having completed a circumnavigation and brought us here safely and with such reliability. We arrived with only 22 litres of water remaining in a drum!

After a refreshing unbroken sleep until late in the morning, Beebee and I went on a quest to find my old painting. Surprisingly it has not been overpainted. I quickly set to repainting it, adding a new broad border on which I painted "AROUND THE WORLD 2015 – 2018", bragging rights can sometimes be justified, well, at the very least this is my opinion.

Horta paintings by visiting sailors

Grace "refreshed" in the Azores

The next few days were spent relaxing and meeting people at the bar, also doing necessary chores like laundry and boat maintenance. The main and staysail were taken down and large patches glued on, preferably when no one was about, so as not to cause me embarrassment!

BEYOND THE SUNSET

32

The Azores to Gibraltar

The boat yard, which was incorporated within the marina offered a service where they would lift a boat out of the water using a travel lift and hold it in the slings. This would give the owner the opportunity to clean the bottom and remove barnacles and marine growth. They allowed 2 hours for this work and then the boat would be put back in the water and the cost for this service was surprisingly inexpensive.

I took advantage of this service and spent a very satisfying 2 hours scraping off barnacles which so cruelly had stolen our speed over the weeks causing added problems with food and water shortages. We stayed overnight in the boatyard dock, leaving Horta at 07:00 hours, bound for Gibraltar, having completed our outward clearance the day before.

My first entry in the log on our first day, the 21st April 2018 states that the wind is very light N W and we are motor-sailing, doing 4.5 knots at 800 rpm. Our speed is so much improved after getting rid of the barnacles! The Gibraltar weigh-point is 1,090 miles from our position.

At 16:00 hours we are sailing without the engine,

effortlessly in the light wind, proving the difference a clean bottom makes. I curse the man who sold me the "very good paint" in the Richards Bay boat yard. Aries is also steering without fault, backing up what I have always thought that a fouled bottom makes self-steering very difficult.

On Sunday, at 09:00 hours we are making 5 knots on a light northerly wind. The sea is flat and the sky is overcast and grey. Our noon run is 88 miles, quite good considering that we barely made steerage in the very light wind overnight. My log entry at 17:00 hours states we are now 971 miles from Gibraltar. I am really enjoying the sail with Grace gliding so serenely over these flat seas, and so pleased to be on our way again.

Monday 23rd April 2018 Day3
07:00 hours N 38 19 W 24 54
Gibraltar 923 miles
wind 10 – 12 knots sea light grey overcast steering 100 T

By mid-morning the sun has come out and we are moving well at 5 knots in the 12 knot wind which is on our beam, a favourite point of sail for Grace.

It is such a luxury having plenty of water again as well as bread, jam, sugar, cheese and fresh vegetables on board. I have kept my habit of not having or drinking alcohol at sea. Aries continues to work well and Beebee has settled into her ocean mode quite contentedly and seems to accept this ocean way of life as normal existence. Our noon run is 86 miles, so different from previous weeks.

On Thursday, the 26th of April, our sixth day I record that the previous four days have given us low mileages, due to the very light winds and calms these past few days. Could this be the start of the Azores High Pressure Zone which kept me worried for those weeks.

Friday 27th April 2018 Day 7

09:00 hours N 37 27 W 18 37

Run 88 miles

wind 10 – 15 knots raining sea flat making 5 knots

Our noon run is 88 miles and we are 600 miles from the Gibraltar straights.

The next morning, our 8th day at sea the wind has come up fresh at 20-25 knots bringing with it a very rough sea, our first since leaving the Azores. We are treble reefed, making over 6 knots. This change in the weather had been forecasted to me by Marilyn, so was not unexpected.

At noon our recorded run is 112 miles but the wind is still freshening. By late afternoon it has become too strong for Aries to steer Grace, leaving me no choice but to set the sails to the heave-to position. We are now being driven to lea at about 2 knots and as many times in the past, Grace is quite comfortable with this.

I kept us hove-to through the night and by Sunday morning we are once again underway, albeit treble reefed in a squally wind. The day is overcast, cold and grey, but the sea has much improved from the previous night. Our noon run is 64 miles, a lot due to our strong easterly drift whilst being hove-to, which was in the preferred direction.

Monday 30th April 2018 Day 10

08:00 hours N 37 12 W 18 32

Run 81 miles

wind N W 10 – 15 knots sunny moderate sea

heading 110 T making 5 knots Gibraltar 371 miles

Last night was very cold with light changing winds, so I was quite surprised at our 81 miles noon run, after yesterday's difficulties.

I record in the log at 17:00 hours that today's sail has been a very pleasant sailing day which was most enjoyable, due to having lots of sun and a co-operative wind.

Tuesday is proving to be even better, once again lots of sun and an amazing 110 miles run. The sea is flat and the wind remains a steady 10 – 12 knots. We are 232 miles from the Gibraltar weigh-point and the time has come where I must position Grace to avoid the incoming and outgoing shipping traffic as the frequency of shipping is not without danger in the vicinity of Cape Vicente for small boats like Grace, being under-powered and under-crewed. Fortunately, the shipping is also aware of the dangers in this bottleneck and so keeps good watches, which is not always the case in the open ocean!

Wednesday, our 12th day at sea, finds us sailing at 2 knots in the very light winds on a flat sea. The weather is mild and we are enjoying some sun. I am pleased with our 72 miles run, quite surprised in fact, because of the very light overnight winds, which barely gave us steerage. Around noon the wind disappeared completely so I am obliged to run the motor at idle speed. I am in very good spirits today because Gibraltar, the official beginning and end of the circumnavigation sail, is less than 200 miles away and with any luck and God's blessing, I shall be home in less than a month.

Thursday 3rd May 2018 Day 13
06:00 hours N 26 12 W 08 41
run 69 miles
wind N 8-10 knots sea choppy sunny

The previous evening and night we were frustrated with no wind and so drifted until 01:00 hours, when the wind reappeared and we were soon making 4 knots in a promising breeze from the north east. Our heading is 100 degrees true and we are windward sailing. At dawn the wind swung to the west picking up to 12-15 knots and giving us a 5 knots speed downwind on a run.

At 19:30 hours I took a photograph of the setting sun, this being my last Atlantic night on Grace and so my final Atlantic sunset. This is also the last 100 miles of my circumnavigation and excitement is building within me at the prospect of the entering the Mediterranean Sea again.

BEYOND THE SUNSET

Friday 4th May 2018
06:00 hours N 36 02 W 06 42
Run 97 miles
wind 0-5 knots sea flat high cloud
Gibraltar 42 miles
motoring 4.9 knots at 750 RPM

The wind over night was very light but we managed to keep steering and I am pleased at 06:00 hours to see that our Gibraltar way point which is at the entrance is now only 42 miles away.

Late last night a message came through from Marilyn on my tracker warning me of a strong easterly head wind. This is expected early Sunday morning and will blow throughout the day. From previous experience I know that easterlies in the Gibraltar Straights can be very strong, blowing at gale force at times and often lasting for days on end. So, because of this forecast I know I must get anchored in Gibraltar before midnight on Saturday or otherwise wait it out in Tarifa. Tarifa is a small town at the entrance to the Gibraltar Straights where in 2007 on my way back from the West Indies I was forced to wait out a strong easterly which lasted 5 days.

Currently, my AIS radar is showing a continuous flow of shipping traffic in and out of the Straights at times I see up to 12 ships at once within ten miles of our position. This calls for great care from me and a constant eye on the radar. It is quite frightening when a ship looms up on my stern, sometime requiring me to call it on the

VHF radio to make sure it is aware of my presence. The response is usually rapid and polite, in the affirmative because these large ships are also exercising great care in this ocean bottle neck of shipping. My last Atlantic log entry reads: "*This approach to Gibraltar is the last day in the Atlantic Ocean on Grace, the last 25 miles of a 27,000 mile circumnavigation. Beebee and I are already enjoying long walks, on clouds of course. I have no sadness of the sail coming to an end but rather I look forward to the next chapter of my life spending more time with Marilyn and my family also I look forward to restoring my ever trust worthy Grace and Beebee and I living a quieter life in my house in Kefalonia*".

At noon we find ourselves only 9 miles from the entrance to the Gibraltar Straights and 36 miles from Gibraltar. The wind is picking up and is now blowing 20 knots from the SSE which is giving us a good speed in the last few miles of the Atlantic Ocean.

I have decided to stop at Tarifa for a few hours' sleep, before pressing on to Gibraltar as the last 24 hours has left me exhausted and I will be tackling the Straights in the dark. It is best not to do this without some rest but not forgetting that the easterly wind is forecast early Sunday morning, which has also been confirmed by Tarifa traffic control radio on their hourly weather forecast.

At 18:00 hours I dropped the anchor in a little bay just before Tarifa town. Beebee and I rowed ashore and then walked a short distance to a small supermarket where I bought three beers. On returning to the boat I treated myself to two beers with my dinner. I then put my head down having set the alarm to ring in a couple of hours. After two hours of deep sleep helped by the beers and a full stomach I again lifted the anchor and we set off in the dark, leaving our little bay behind. The wind I noticed with relief, had dropped in strength but not yet swung to the forecasted easterly direction.

I pushed Grace down the straights using the engine and making as much speed from the sails as the wind would allow, ever wary of the expected easterly wind which could arrive at any moment. The excitement of our soon arrival in Gibraltar and the two hours sleep has filled me with fresh energy. All through the night nature remained kind to us and at 03:00 hours I dropped the anchor behind the Spanish breakwater near Alcadeza marina.

We have now officially completed the circumnavigation after two years and eight months and climbing into bed, a feeling of peace and satisfaction was quickly overpowered by the deep necessity to sleep.

In the morning, at around 10am I lifted the anchor and motored Grace into the marina on the Spanish side of Gibraltar which is separated from the "Rock" by the airport runway, considered to be the border between the Spanish and British territories. After the check in procedures Beebee and I walked into Gibraltar town where I e-mailed Marilyn and let her know of our safe arrival. It was heartening to receive many e-mails from family and friends who have been following me on my tracker, which plots my daily position on my website every day, all expressing their congratulations on completing the circumnavigation.

I felt proud to have achieved a long held dream. I posted on my website "*I would like to thank all the people who helped and supported me to achieve my lifelong dream, and also thank all those who gave money to Cancer Research UK. And I would also like to thank Marilyn, who has put up with a lot, for her never failing support. The circumnavigation was all I thought it would be, fascinating places I saw, made special friends, met people that I would not normally meet, lots of hardship and stress but also the most amazing beauty and tranquillity on a lonely ocean under the big sky.*"

33

Gibraltar to Kefalonia

Tuesday 8th May 2018

18:00 hours N 36 25 W 04 58

We left Alcadeza marina at noon, motored across to Gibraltar took on diesel at the fuel dock, the cheapest diesel to be found anywhere, then headed Grace east into the Mediterranean Sea.

The following morning at 11.30 am we find ourselves already 100 miles from Gibraltar. Our speed overnight was very good, often doing 7 knots under double reef sails in the very fresh westerly wind which had picked up shortly after leaving Gibraltar. As Almerimar marina is coming up on my port side I made a quick decision to spend the night there. This marina is a favourite of mine and I have used it many times when transiting the Mediterranean Sea. The facilities here in this very large marina are excellent, having its own supermarket and many bars and restaurants. It is also one of the least expensive marina's in Spain.

Thursday 10th May 2018

After leaving the marina at noon I set course for Carbo de Gata, a prominent peninsula where a very tall conspicuous light house is located. This whole area is part of a beautiful national park.

Rounding the peninsula, we carried on through the night and then anchored at Aquila on Friday afternoon.

Saturday 12th May 2018

After pulling up the anchor at 07:00 hours we sailed on until Tuesday without stopping, as I am eager to keep moving to get home to Kefalonia.

Tuesday morning we arrived at Porto Colom on Majorca part of the Balearic islands, having motored most of the way in the very settled weather conditions. I met up with Geoff again, he and I had spent Christmas together after the dis-masting in 2015. He lives on his boat at anchor in Porto Colom. Whilst there, Geoff helped me fit a new key to the top of my rudder stock, the old one had worn badly making the steering very sloppy.

Thursday 17th May saw us under way again, heading for Sardinia.

I pressed on without stopping until our arrival on Sunday 20th May in Calasetta, on the island of Sardinia, after motoring most of the way from Porto Colom in light to non-existent winds.

After launching the dinghy in the afternoon, Beebee and I went ashore to pick up some groceries and two drums of diesel. Whilst enjoying a beer at a bar with free internet was able to speak to Marilyn on Skype. She remarked on our rapid progress through the Mediterranean but also said she had very sad news for me.

Doug my dear brother, has passed away from a sudden heart attack. I took the news very hard as Doug and I had been close all our lives. He died in his bedroom and was only found the following day. Doug's wife had died in 2010 and they never had any children. He had become reclusive after her death and I would only see him when visiting the UK to see my children and other family members.

I left Calasetta on Monday morning in pouring rain, feeling deeply sad about Doug, motoring towards Cefalu in Sicily.

Dawn of the 24th May found us approaching the anchorage in Cefalu after motoring for three days.

Friday morning we were on our way to the Messina Straights, heaving-to 3 miles north of the city of Messina at sunset. There is no wind so we are drifting and I have decided to wait it out until the morning. It makes more sense to tackle this busy waterway in daylight.

We navigated the straights in fine weather, only stopping for an hour at noon to take on diesel at Reggio de Calabria, a large city on the mainland side of the straights. Leaving Italy we were blessed with a perfect north-west wind and fine weather for the three day crossing to Kefalonia.

I had previously spoken to Marilyn about my arrival in Kefalonia and we had worked out an arrival time and date. She expected about 30 or more people, family and friends who would like to see my arrival in Argostoli. ETA's are notoriously difficult to predict for boats like Grace, so because of this I have decided to arrive the night before and anchor off-shore, two miles from the harbour entrance at a small island which offered good holding and protection. This would ensure that I could bring Grace into the marina at 15:00 hours as previously agreed.

Tuesday 07:30 hours 29th May 2018

N 38 07 E 19 56

My log entry for this morning reads "*We are now 23 miles from Kefalonia. The wind remained light overnight so we managed only 27 miles in 24 hours.*" I expect to anchor at Vardianoi Island before noon. The very familiar mountainous island is now quite visible in front of us. I feel quite euphoric at our imminent arrival but we will have to wait until tomorrow before going into the marina. This will be my last entry in the logbook in my two years and nine months circumnavigation. **I had made a promise to Beebee and Grace to bring them home, so we have done it**!

The familiar mountainous profile of Kefalonia is now clearly visible. I feel euphoric at our imminent arrival but I will have to wait until tomorrow before I bring Grace to the dock in the marina. At around noon we anchored at the island in beautiful sunshine. I felt totally at peace, without a care in the world and spent the afternoon tidying up the boat and preparing for our arrival tomorrow.

On Wednesday the 30th May, I motored Grace in glorious sunshine into the marina at Argostoli. On the dock stood a crowd of well-wishers, including Marilyn, my sister Audrey, who had flown in from England to see my homecoming, plus many friends and associates. There was a lot of shouting and blowing of horns, creating a cacophony of welcoming noise as I brought Grace gently to the dock side. Willing hands took my lines, we were finally home.

I switched off the engine for the last time and Beebee and I stepped ashore to enjoy the wonderful homecoming welcome from Marilyn, Audrey, Marilyn's daughter Rachel and partner Steve and all our friends and well-wishers.

After thanking everybody for creating this special occasion, shaking hands and greeting all individually, I turned and looked at my fifty year old wooden boat. She showed battle scars with rust streaks down her sides, sun-bleached and peeling paint. I quietly blessed and thanked her for ensuring we came home safely, carrying us all these thousands of miles, crossing many oceans and seas so tirelessly always so incredibly safe and reliable.

The End

Epilogue

Audrey my sister

Audrey, my sister passed away in March 2020. She lost her fight against cancer, so cheerfully and bravely waged for over six years. In this time she almost completed a Fine Arts Degree at university but the cancer took from her the chance to finish her final year.

She and I had always been close, as all of we siblings had been throughout our lives. She was my true confidante and best friend. Sadly, I am the sole remaining member of the Malcolm Mine family.

AN AUTOBIOGRAPHY OF
THE CHALLENGE OF
LIFE AND SURVIVAL,
FROM CHILDHOOD TO
OLD AGE, WRITTEN ON
THE BACKGROUND OF A
SOLO SAIL AROUND THE
WORLD WITH A DOG
FOR COMPANY.

Beebee and Malcolm